THE BITE OF THE NIGHT

PLAYSCRIPT 115

THE BITE OF THE NIGHT:
An Education

Howard Barker

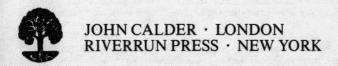

JOHN CALDER · LONDON
RIVERRUN PRESS · NEW YORK

First published in Great Britain, 1988, by
John Calder (Publishers) Limited
18 Brewer Street, London W1R 4AS

and in the United States of America, 1988, by
Riverrun Press Inc
1170 Broadway, New York, NY 10001

All performing rights in this play are strictly reserved and applications for performance should be made to:

Judy Daish Associates Limited
83 Eastbourne Mews, London W2 6LQ

No performance of this play may be given unless a licence has been obtained prior to rehearsal.

British Library Cataloguing in Publicaton Data
Barker, Howard, *1946* –
 The bite of the night : an education. —
 (Playscript; 115).
 I. Title
 822'.914

ISBN 0-7145-4124-9

Library of Congress Cataloging-in-Publication Data

Barker, Howard.
 The bite of the night : an education / Howard Barker.
 96p. 19.8cm. — (Playscript : 115)
 ISBN 0-7145-4124-9
 I. Title. II. Series.
PR6052.A6485B58 1988
822'.914 — dc19   88-18529
                                                                    CIP

Data manipulaton and photocomposition in 9 on 10 point Times Roman by Artset (London) Ltd. (A division of the Image Communications Group)
Printed in Great Britain by Hillman Printers (Frome) Ltd., Somerset

To Tony Dunn

'All is True'

(Title of play ascribed to Shakespeare)

'Beauty is not truth, but the best available lie on the subject of truth. . .'
(Act 3, *The Bite of the Night*)

'Every man's evil expresses me.'

(Poem 13, *The Breath of the Crowd*)

THE BITE OF THE NIGHT was first performed by The Royal Shakespeare Company at The Pit, Barbican, London, on the 31 August 1988, with the following cast:

MACLUBY, a soap boiler	Clive Russell
CREUSA, a woman of Troy	Darlene Johnson
SAVAGE, a scholar	Nigel Terry
BOY, his son	Jimmy Gallagher
OLD MAN, his parent	Jimmy Gardner
HOGBIN, his pupil	David O'Hara
HELEN, a defector	Diane Fletcher
FLADDER, her husband, King of the Greeks	Michael Cadman
GUMMERY, a soldier	Gordon Case
EPSOM, a soldier	Steven Elliot
SHADE, a soldier	Sean Baker
A BOY, of Troy	Jimmy Gallagher
GAY, a daughter of Helen	Janet Amsbury
HOMER, a poet	Mark Dignam
BOY, son of Savage (adult)	Jimmy Gallagher
ASAFIR, a Truce official	David Pullen
YORAKIM, a Truce official	Ian Bailey
JOHN, their servant	Richard Leaf
CHARITY, daughter of Gay	Marya Spiers/Gemma Green
SCHLIEMANN, an archaeologist	John Carlisle
YORAKIM, a labourer	Ian Bailey
ASAFIR, a labourer	David Pullen
OFFICERS	Patrick Cremin, Gordon Warnecke
YOUTHS	Richard Leaf
PUBLIC	

Designed by	Kandis Cook
Directed by	Danny Boyle

First Prologue

MACLUBY. They brought a woman from the street
    And made her sit in the stalls
    By threats
    By bribes
    By flattery
    Obliging her to share a little of her life with actors

    But I don't understand art

    Sit still, they said

    But I don't want to see sad things

    Sit still, they said

    And she listened to everything
    Understanding some things
    But not others
    Laughing rarely, and always without knowing why
    Sometimes suffering disgust
    Sometimes thoroughly amazed
    And in the light again said

    If that's art I think it is hard work
    It was beyond me
    So much of it beyond my actual life

    But something troubled her
    Something gnawed her peace
    And she came a second time, armoured with friends

    Sit still, she said

    And again, she listened to everything
    This time understanding different things
    This time untroubled that some things
    Could not be understood
    Laughing rarely but now without shame
    Sometimes suffering disgust

Sometimes thoroughly amazed
And in the light again said

That is art, it is hard work

And one friend said, too hard for me
And the other said if you will
I will come again

Because I found it hard I felt honoured

Second Prologue

**It is not true that everyone wants to be
Entertained
Some want the pain of unknowing**
Shh
Shh
Shh
The ecstasy of not knowing for once
The sheer suspension of not knowing
Shh
Shh
Shh
Three students in a smoke-filled room
Three girls on holiday
A pregnancy on a Saturday night
I knew that
I knew that
I already knew that

The marriage which was hardly
The socialist who wasn't
The American with the plague
I knew that
I knew that
I already knew that

We can go home now
Oh, car seat kiss my arse
We can go home now
Oh, underground upholstery
Caress my buttock
I loved that play it was so true
Take your skirt off
I loved that play it was so

Take your skirt off
What are theatres for
Take your skirt off

This has to be the age for more musicals
Declares the manager
The people are depressed

This has to be the age for more musicals
Declares the careerist
Who thinks the tilted face is power
Who believes humming is believing

No
The problems are different
They are
They really are
I say this with all the circumspection
A brute can muster

I ask you
Hatred apart
Abuse apart
Boredom in abeyance
Politics in the cupboard
Anger in the drawer
Should we not

I know it's impossible but you still try

Not reach down beyond the known for once

I'll take you
I'll hold your throat
I will
And vomit I will tolerate
Over my shirt
Over my wrists
Your bile
Your juices
I'll be your guide
And whistler in the dark
Cougher over filthy words
And all known sentiments recycled for this house

Clarity
Meaning
Logic
And Consistency

None of it
None

I honour you too much
To paste you with what you already know so

Beyond the slums of England
Tower blocks floating on ponds of urine
Like the lighthouse on its bed of mercury

Beyond the screams of women fouled
Who have lost sight and sense of all desire

And grinning classes of male satirists
Beyond
The witty deconstruction of the literary myth
And individuals in the web of class

No ideology on the cheap
No ideology on the cheap

You think a thing repeated three times is a truth
You think to sing along is solidarity

No ideology on the cheap

Apologies
Old spasms
Apologies
Old temper
Apologies
Apologies

I charm you
Like the Viennese professor in the desert
Of America
My smile is a crack of pain
Like the exiled pianist in the tart's embrace
My worn fingers reach for your place
Efficiently

It's an obligation ... !

ACT ONE

Scene One

The Ruins of a University

CREAUSA. Lost in Troy. (*Pause*.) Listen, getting lost. (*Pause*.) That also is
an infidelity (*Pause*.) I walked behind. Wife bearing the food. The flask.
The diapers. Wife under the bundle. The clock. The colander. The old
man's vests. Through flaming alleys by clots of rapists whose glistening
arses caught the light. The chess set and the fruit cake. Wives under the
soldiers. The flannel and the toothbrushes (*Pause*.)
Turks in Smyrna
Romans in Carthage
Scots in Calais
Swedes in Dresden
Goths in Buda
Japs in Nanking
Russians in Brandenburg

Unbelted and unbuttoned they thrust their arms
into the well of skirt

I did prefer
I did
To continuing this marriage in another place
Prefer to get lost
The gutters bubbling with semen notwithstanding
The spontaneous stabblings of intoxicated looters
Notwithstanding
I slipped down Trader's Avenue and hid

And he came back
I I will say this
I will give credit where it's
He did
He did come back
A dozen paces boy in hand and dad on back
His eyes shouted
His mouth hung speechless as a ripped sheet

I could have
I wanted to
That grey and never happy face

Creu — sa!

Once my name heaved out his gob and stuck to
Falling arches
Once
His last call
Only once
It drifted down with burning papers
It sailed on draughts like embers of old frocks

And turned away
Triangle of males
The three degrees of man

I vomited my shame into the shop
On all smashed things I added pounds of self disgust
And wiping on a dead man's curtain stood up frail
But light

Widowhood is grief but also chance
And falls of cities both finishes and starts

Scene Two

A MAN *and* A CHILD

SAVAGE. **I will end up killing you.**
BOY. Yes.
SAVAGE. I think we know that, don't we? I will end up killing you?
BOY. Yes.
SAVAGE. And burying you in the coke. Under the power station floor. Or
　　sling you in a rusty truck...
BOY. Yes.
SAVAGE. One eye hanging from some almighty blow. **We do know that,
　　don't we?**
BOY. Yes.
SAVAGE (*sits*). Through no fault of your own...
BOY. Not really, no...
SAVAGE. My character being what it is. And the times being what they are.
　　The state of the world and my temper. I think murdering you is inevitable.
　　Kiss me. (THE BOY *kisses him.*)
BOY. You have to have freedom.
SAVAGE. I must have it. I am forty and I must have it.

BOY. Everything's against you.

SAVAGE. Every fucking thing.

BOY. And I'm a constant irritation.

SAVAGE. Not constant.

BOY. Not constant, but an irritation.

SAVAGE. Children are.

BOY. We are, and then there's grandad. We're both an irritation and we are obviously holding up freedom.

SAVAGE. Yes...

BOY. You're forty and freedom's like a muscle, if it isn't used it at — it at —

SAVAGE. Shut up.

BOY. It atrophies —

SAVAGE. **Shut up.** (*Pause.*) Kiss me. Kiss me! (THE BOY *kisses him.* AN OLD MAN *enters with a pot.*)

OLD MAN. Done the potatoes.

BOY. What does atrophy mean?

OLD MAN. Done the potatoes.

SAVAGE. Oh, the gnawed bone of my mind...the bloody, gnawed bone of my mind... (*Pause. They look at him.*) Dirty butcher's bone in the gutter no dog would stoop to lick... (*Pause.*)

BOY. You always say that.

SAVAGE. I do. I do say that

BOY. You put your hands to your head and you say the gnawed bone of my mind...

SAVAGE. Yes...

BOY. What's the matter with it?

OLD MAN. Lucky to find potatoes... (*He goes off.*)

SAVAGE. I woke in the night. I woke in the night and the sky was purple with the bruise of cities. I thought of avenues where they sleep the sleep of family love, the pillowcase, the nightdress, the twitching of the poodle. **You call that life?**

BOY. Call that life?

SAVAGE. The dozing daughter in the dormitory town has tossed off the eiderdown. Down it goes, hiss to the nylon carpet and piles like warm shit from the sphincter of the dog. **You call that life?**

BOY. Call that life?

SAVAGE. Every dead clerk is a slab on the causeway to liberty.

BOY. Down with clerks! Down with documents!

SAVAGE. I taught Homer here... (HOGBIN *enters.*)

HOGBIN. Sorry I'm late. (*Pause.*) Am I late? (*Pause.*) Am I sorry? (*He sits.*) I had an excuse, and then I thought, he does not care if I have an excuse or not. I thought in fact, if I do not appear he will not notice, so I would only demean myself by inventing an excuse in the first place. Why appear at all, in fact? **Homeric fucking Greece, what does that say to me?** Sitting on the bus this was, at the back eye-deep in soup of fags and women's underwear. **Homeric fucking Greece?**

SAVAGE. You barren filth.

HOGBIN. Now, then...

SAVAGE. You ephemeral spewing of suburban couplings.

HOGBIN. Of course I am ephemeral. So are we all.

SAVAGE. Abuse and more abuse.

HOGBIN. *Merci.* I didn't do the essay. But here's the notes.

SAVAGE. The notes?

BOY. He doesn't want your notes!

HOGBIN. I heard the reggae through the wall. The beat bored into me. I looked at Homer. Dead letters swum before my eyes. Old Europe struggling with the beat. The beat! The fucking beat! **Give us knowledge, Doctor Savage!** (*Pause.*)

SAVAGE. The Trojan War. (*Pause.*) The Trojan War occurred because a married woman lent her body to a stranger. (*Pause.*) That's all for today. (*Pause.*)

HOGBIN. I knew that.

SAVAGE. Excellent.

HOGBIN. **I knew that, git.**

SAVAGE. You read it. You did not know it. Knowledge is belief. (*He gets up to go.*)

HOGBIN. **Don't get up.** (*Pause.*) The seduction of Helen. The seduction of Helen is a metaphor for the commercial success of the tribes of Asia Minor and the subsequent collapse of the Peloponnesian carrying trade. Only a military alliance of the Greek states restored the monopoly. In classical fashion the outcome of trade wars is the enslavement of populations in the interests of cost-free labour and the eradication of the infrastructure of the rival enterprise, namely the razing of cities. (*Pause.*)

SAVAGE. No. It was cunt.

HOGBIN. Cunt's the metaphor, trade's the —

SAVAGE. **Helen's cunt.** (*Pause.*)

SAVAGE. That's it for today, Mr Hogbin. (*Pause.*)

HOGBIN. I hate my father. He is a big-bollocked snob who walks the streets in shorts and stares at women. Intellectuals he calls bums. Bums, he calls them. He has foreign holidays and speaks American. What does bums mean? Bums means arses but I think he means tramps. **Give us your intuitions and stuff the facts.** (*Pause. He gets up.*) Cunt, was it… (*He goes out. MACLUBY enters, looks at SAVAGE, describes:*)

MACLUBY. Been crouching here since the final tutorial. The door shut and they left. Down slid the timetable with the rust. The tinkling of drawing pins, the descent of postcards. Then the lampshade crashed. The splintering of fluorescent lances in cracked corridors. The mole's disdain of plastic tiles. And then the landscape yawned, and chalk breathed out, undoing the keystone of the library arch. **We all heard the Library crash.**

SAVAGE. I heard it.

BOY. I heard it! Books blew everywhere!

MACLUBY. And you stayed put. While demolition cowboys ripped the wiring out.

SAVAGE. **Knowledge!**

MACLUBY. While they smashed the basins kept your seat.

SAVAGE. **Knowledge!**

MACLUBY. Their curses, their pornographic sentiments.

SAVAGE. **Knowledge!**

MACLUBY. The clatter of their arid minds and mundane politics.

SAVAGE (*pause*). It was a paper overcoat against their spit... (THE BOY *holds* SAVAGE.) I lost his mother. She could not stomach me. My whine and bite. My sitting on the edge of the chair. **Put your arse back in the chair!** I could not. My whine and bite...

MACLUBY. Give us the kid. (*Pause.*)

SAVAGE. Give you the —

MACLUBY. Give us him, why don't you? (*Pause.*)

SAVAGE. Who are —

MACLUBY. Harry MacLuby. Soap boiler.

SAVAGE. Soap boiler?

MACLUBY. Well, do you want him or not? (*Pause.*) On your sick bed, writhing like a worm on baking bricks, shouting the whole length of the ward, **I did nothing with my life, because of them, they weighed on me.** Your cry of misery would lift the gutters off the hospital... (*Pause.*)

SAVAGE. **Soap boiler...?**

MACLUBY. Ashes of Roses. (*Pause.*)

SAVAGE. My mother ditched me also...

MACLUBY. There you go...

SAVAGE. A poor boy will find his benefactress...

MACLUBY. Inevitably, and what use are you?

SAVAGE. No use...

MACLUBY. All your kisses papered over hate...

SAVAGE. **I drink his fondness and resent his life.**

MACLUBY. You know, you see, you do know...

SAVAGE. Love of children, what is it? Self-love. The clinging of a desperate mortality. You have to understand the feeling. Not just feel the feeling or you are a mollusc. What are you, a murderer?

MACLUBY. Silly.

SAVAGE. And in five years he will not lend me one stale breath...

MACLUBY. It's so, it is...

MACLUBY (*to* THE BOY). **This man wants you.**

BOY. Wants me?

SAVAGE. He says.

BOY. What for?

SAVAGE. Apprentice in the soap trade.

BOY. Soap?

SAVAGE. **Soap, Yes, Soap!** (*Pause.*) Get your things. (*Pause.*)

BOY. I think, in spite of everything, although you will probably murder me, I would prefer to stay with —

SAVAGE. Toothbrush. Flannel. And clean pants.

BOY. Rather die from you bashing me in one of your fits than —

SAVAGE. Pyjamas if you've got some —

BOY. **Live with anybody else.** (*Pause.* SAVAGE *refuses to look at him.*) **I love you.**

SAVAGE. Love, he says. That word. Emaciated syllable. (*He looks at him.*)
Replace the word love with another. And you will see how thin it is.
BOY. There is no other.
SAVAGE. **Mollusc!**
BOY. You are always calling me a mollusc...
SAVAGE. Yes... (*Pause.*)
BOY. You are so unhappy. And I can't help... (*Pause, then* THE BOY *goes off.*)
SAVAGE. You see, how I have become his child, and he is burdened with me.
I make him suffer for me. (*He looks at* MACLUBY.) Teach him Ashes of
Roses. The man who can smother mortality in scent, or wash blood off
the hands of killers will not lack for friends. (THE OLD MAN *enters with
a plate of dinner. He looks at* SAVAGE, *pitying him.*)
OLD MAN (*to* MACLUBY). I said to him, travel. Travel the world, go on.
MACLUBY. He hates the world...
OLD MAN. The merchant navy, for example. See things while you have the
power.
MACLUBY. The Taj Mahal. The pyramids...
OLD MAN. The Taj Mahal. The pyramids...
SAVAGE. The truth is not in all that junk, you —
MACLUBY. Old Moscow's onion domes... (THE BOY *returns, with a small
bag. He stands waiting.* SAVAGE *looks at him, suddenly weeps.* THE
BOY *goes to touch him.*)
SAVAGE. No...! (*Pause, then* MACLUBY *leads the way and* THE BOY
follows. Pause.)
OLD MAN. Football, is it? (*He puts the plate down, starts to go.*)
SAVAGE. I owe you nothing, do I? (*He stops.*) Because you grated on my
mother, what's the debt?
OLD MAN. No debt, son.
SAVAGE. And because one not-so-very-mad night I squirmed against his
mother, to the ticking of the wedding present and the clatter of the
drunkards in the sick-swamped street, so setting in motion the torture of
paternity, **I owe no debt, me neither, do I?** (*Pause.*) Argue. Argue for your
rights to me.
OLD MAN. No rights.
SAVAGE. No rights... (THE OLD MAN *turns to leave again.*) And what is
intimacy anyway?
OLD MAN. Search me...
SAVAGE. I clung to her and it was two pebbles clashing. (THE OLD MAN
looks.) When I was in her, hard against her womb, some razor slashed my
head, some miniature blade designed to kill conception **you don't expect
to find knives in there of all places.** Anyway, it failed, and he was born...
OLD MAN (*nodding after* THE BOY). Football today, is it? (*A hiatus of
pity.*) Did I ever thank you for the books?
SAVAGE. Books?
OLD MAN. On Homeric Metre. By Dr Savage of the University. To My
Father on that great big empty page.
SAVAGE. Christ knows why I —

OLD MAN. An Introduction to the Iliad. In Memory of My Mother.

SAVAGE. Barmy reflex of a clever son —

OLD MAN. No, I —

SAVAGE. **Don't lick feeling off that line of arid print.** (*Pause.*)

OLD MAN. Wha'? (*Pause.*)

SAVAGE. The binding was so poor the leaves fell out. As if they were ashamed to hang with such a dedication —

OLD MAN. Wha'?

SAVAGE. **The sentimental liar I have been.**

OLD MAN. Kind thought I thought...

SAVAGE. Kind thought? I hated you. Your mundane opinions. Your repetition of half-truths. Straddling my back. You burden. You dead weight. **He's gone so why don't you.** (THE OLD MAN *turns.*) No one is here for long. Who knows, some death might be already on me. Some growth in the dark, deep wet. Give us some time for my own needs. Old bones. Old pelt. (THE OLD MAN *withdraws some yards behind* SAVAGE, *and sits.*) We can have knowledge, but not in passivity. Knowledge exists, but the path is strewn with obstacles. (THE OLD MAN *breaks the plate.*) These obstacles we ourselves erect. (*He takes a shard.*) The conspiracy of the ignorant against the visionary can be broken only by the ruthless intellect. (*He undoes his vest.*) Pity also is a regime. (*He attempts to cut his throat.*) And consideration a manacle.

OLD MAN. Trying...

SAVAGE. Manners —

OLD MAN. Trying...

SAVAGE. Loyalty —

OLD MAN. Trying, fuck it —

SAVAGE. Responsibility, **iron bands on the brain.** (HOGBIN *enters with a book.*)

HOGBIN. Helen was a whore in any case, it says — (*He sees* THE OLD MAN.) Oi.

SAVAGE. **Knowledge is beyond kindness you know —**

HOGBIN. **Oi!**

SAVAGE. Shut up... (THE OLD MAN *succeeds, gurgles.*)

HOGBIN. Hey! Fucking hey!

SAVAGE. I know. I know he is. (HOGBIN *stares at him.* THE OLD MAN *dies.* SAVAGE *suddenly seizes* HOGBIN, *in a horrified embrace.*) **Kiss me, then! My triumph! Kiss me, then!**

HOGBIN. Oh, fucking —

SAVAGE. **Kiss me!**

HOGBIN. Oh, bloody 'ell —

SAVAGE. **My liberty! My appalling liberty!**

HOGBIN (*tearing from his embrace*). Oh, shit and shit —

SAVAGE. Don't leave me.

HOGBIN. **He — lp**

SAVAGE (*grasping him tightly*). Did it...did it...did it. (*They rock to and fro. Pause.*)

HOGBIN. Blood's tickling my toes...warm tickle...old man's contents...old man's drain...(*He shudders.*)

OLD MAN. We left the lorry on the road, looking for crashed bombers on the scarp, sun in, sun out, behind these towering clouds and dark drenches of rain, I was alone and saw the tailplane in a smudge of trees, or wing was it, with roundels of the R.A.F., and my boots went swish towards it, swish through downland flowers while the wind creaked faintly in the beached boughs of the thorny trees, alone and hot, smell of tunic, smell of blanco, swish went the poppy heads, alone and hot **up shot like rabbits from a dip two naked arses** brown as polish, gipsies fucking to the rhythm of that wing in scattered tracer belts and navigation clocks, swish the pelting of their feet, leaving her arse print in the turf, her shoulder blades were printed in the turf until with little jerks the grass stood up again. (*Pause.*)

SAVAGE. The death of my father necessitates the cancellation of our next tutorial.

HOGBIN. For grief, is that?

SAVAGE. Grief, yes.

HOGBIN. The socialized consequence of death is naturally bereavement but under grief the individual might conceal some inexplicable delight. (*Pause.*) I pose the question only —

SAVAGE. **I said you hungry adolescent no tutorial.**

HOGBIN. Not a tutorial, no, but —

SAVAGE. My old man's dead, whose dry hand was the only proof of goodness I knew yet, I carried him through Troy! (*Pause.*) 'To think my boy taught brilliance here', he said, to reprimand the red-backed bastards ripping off the roof. He never read books but still he hated televisions, he chucked them out the windows of the flats, some instinct he had for shattering mendacity, the incorruptible old sod...

HOGBIN. The spontaneity of violence is surely the formal resistance of the proletariat to —

SAVAGE. **Won't teach.** (*He goes to arrange* THE OLD MAN.)

HOGBIN. Give us yer handkerchief... (SAVAGE *gives him a rag. He wipes the blood from his feet.*)

SAVAGE. I'm sorry I was born, and sorry I was cured, sorry I fell in love, and sorry I was married, sorry and sorry again for every choice I —

HOGBIN (*wiping himself*). Yeah, but was it choice? You presuppose the possibility of refusals —

SAVAGE. Oh, you arid youth, I think the young are barren as a shaft of concrete in Sahara sun.

HOGBIN. Bollocks, you rhetorical shitter —

SAVAGE. **Wisdom**, not cleverness, **Knowledge**, not retorts, **Truth**, not wit. One bit of truth felt in the veins!

HOGBIN. You are a pile of metred drivel, why I sit here fuck knows, when —

SAVAGE. One truth! One truth! **Not a lot to ask is it!**

HOGBIN. Read Buka on the nature of hyperbole, it's 'ere somewhere — (*He pulls filthy pages from a pocket.* SAVAGE *kicks it across the floor.*)

SAVAGE. **Got to suffer!**

HOGBIN (*gathering the precious pages*). You are a plastic bag of urine —
SAVAGE. **Suffer, youth!**
HOGBIN. Tossed against a corrugated fence — there, now I'm doin' it.
(MACLUBY *appears. Pause.*)
MACLUBY. I gave the boy a ball. His eyes went big. He's nine and he can't
catch.
SAVAGE. I hate balls. The ball returns the idea after every revolution. No
effort, no struggle of the intellect. Give him a polygon to kick.
(MACLUBY *turns to go.*) **A father also loves but through a grating.** Tell
him that...

Scene Three

HELEN *with* A HUSBAND, *seated.*

HELEN. I'm back. (*Pause.*) My arse in the marital chair. (*Pause.*) My piss
in the marital pan. (*Pause.*) **Well, be delighted.** (*Pause.*) You ache to touch
me, but you won't. And silence is your knife. Twist away! (*Pause.*) Troy
was full of intellectuals. I saw their corpses. Their corpses hung on wires.
Do hit me if you want to, others did. (*Pause.*) And all of them kept diaries,
always their diaries in a miniature hand like lice had crept through
inkwells **Any paltry thought they deemed immortal.** Fevered note-takers
and every scrap was burned by troops, every leaf! (*Pause.*)The comedy of
history. (*Pause.*) **Burst my face or I shall go on talking.** (*Pause.*) I saw one
on his knees to drunken squaddies who said not **Spare my life,** not like the
shopkeeper who offered to reveal his hidden loot, not like the civil servant
who offered them his wife to whip to pulp, but **I beg you smuggle out this
book.** I saw the thing kicked down a gutter, the pages bound in fat and
sweat, the banality, the futility! **I am philistine and loveless...** (*Pause.*)
FLADDER. Helen fucks the wounded in the wards, they said. (*Pause.*)
Which aroused me. **Shamefully.** (*Pause.*) Or dogs, some ventured to sug-
gest. Which aroused me. **Shamefully.** (*Pause.*) The filthy infantry. The
long lick of their dreams. (*Pause.*) I crept to the canvas in the dew, sodden
and erect, to eavesdrop what malpractice their knotted maleness would
inflict on you. (*Pause.*) Our suffering. Our ecstasy. (SOLDIERS *enter,
with* CREUSA)
GUMMERY. Every light bulb. Every cage bird.
SHADE/EPSOM. **Pulver!**
GUMMERY. Pity was our banner, as you wrote in final orders. So the tarts
we spared...
EPSOM. And infants, if they did not cry too loud.
GUMMERY. Troy's gone. Nothing to block the wind off Asia now.
Arseholes to this bitch. I must say that. (*He bows to* HELEN.) Your ser-
vant, etcetera.
SHADE. Ten years goes by in a flash...
EPSOM. That final bulge made my heart sink. I never smelled depression
like it, even in defeat. It hung over the trenches like a fog, and the

champagne corks were miserable squibs. No one could work up any speeches, we drifted past old weapon pits and put our lips against the hinges of burnt tanks. Go home? My wife is fucking with the priest, I had it from my brother. What did he think, I'd put a pistol in my gob and make him heir to seven dirty acres? Not that I blame him. Nor the priest, him neither. I blame no one. **Arseholes to this bitch however.** (*He bows to* HELEN.) I must say that. (*He sits on the floor.*)

CREUSA (*looking at her*). Helen...!

FLADDER (*pause*). The word. (*Pause.*) **Helen**. (*Pause.*) The idea. (*Pause.*) **Helen**. (*Pause.*)

CREUSA. Alive...!

FLADDER. She stinks like a horse. I say this, I announce this, I announce this because the idea has got round she is ethereal. No, I assure you it is not the case. I know she stood naked on the battlements in the seventh year —

GUMMERY. The eighth —

FLADDER. The eighth year, was it, stood naked and the wind sneaked round her parts, the cool wind out the Caucasus, fresh with snow and hibiscus, but still she had the odour of the mare, why did you do that? The army laughed, seeing you less than perfect. Seeing your body rather flawed. Of course they knew the sex is not in the proportions, but still they laughed, calling the cooks out of their tents, staring and jabbering, why did she do that? (*Pause.*)

CREUSA. I've been passed round a bit myself.. .not bad...not the worst thing in the world, to have no choice. (*Pause.*) Not the worst thing.

EPSOM (*nudging his neighbour*). Oi...

CREUSA. The worst thing is —

GUMMERY (*indicating* FLADDER, *who weeps*). Oi...

CREUSA. To imagine choice exists... (*Two of the soldiers go to* FLADDER *placing their hands on his shoulders.*)

HELEN. Oh, the solidarity of weeping men... (HOGBIN *enters, stops.*)

HOGBIN. Europe's a mess... (*They look at him.*) I say the only ideology is total scepticism... That's not an ideology, he says. (*He looks them over.*) What's this...? (*They examine him.*) This is a university, so point yer firearms downwards, there's a love... (*They make no move.*) What's this...? (*Pause. He is undeterred.*) Ruins or not, it's still a seat of learning, and so is any place where questions are still asked. Balls to chancellors, and piss on economics, **The Trojans did not scatter,** why should we? Some remained, he says so, fat guts says they fucked their conquerors, **Message for the oppressed!** (SAVAGE *enters.* HOGBIN *bows mockingly.*) The wobbling residue of culture! (*He rises.*) He imitates the amoeba, which cannot be squashed by jeeps.

HELEN. I know him.

HOGBIN. She knows you...!

HELEN. Staggering through courtyards under books. Boiled in your sweat. A stew of anger and unhealthy fat...

HOGBIN. She knows you...!

HELEN. And looking along the wires of dangling intellects I thought, the fat one has escaped my husband's spite...

SAVAGE. Eventually the camps will shut, and rusty execution sheds fall down in gales, and guards retire to plant begonias, **All forgotten!** (*Pause.*) But one still excavates the files, plucks memoirs out of bonfires, and keeps testimony safe in his archival head... (EPSOM *moves to threaten* SAVAGE, *who shrinks to the ground.*) Don't spill the head! (EPSOM *stops, bemused.*) It contains the agony of others, like a cup... (*He looks up.*) You are Helen of Troy... (*She weeps suddenly, cradling him in her arms.*)

HELEN. Yes...and now...obscurity...! (*Pause.* SHADE *picks up his kit.*)

SHADE. Home, James...!

FLADDER. Home?

SHADE. Bands playing on the quay. And similar shit. Flags in babies' gobs. And similar shit. (*To* CREUSA.) Carry my loot, you!

FLADDER. This is home.

SHADE. Wha'?

FLADDER. Where so much hate has concentrated, that must be home also.

SHADE (*to* CREUSA). Mind my mirror!

GUMMERY. **It's home he says.** (SHADE *stops.*)

SHADE. Wha'? (*Pause.*)

GUMMERY. I never knew a Trojan, nor heard of Troy. And yet, no sooner had my boot touched Trojan pebble but —

FLADDER. You hated.

GUMMERY. Just like that. Peculiar.

SAVAGE. Not peculiar. (*Pause. They look at him.*)

HOGBIN. Careful, clever...

SAVAGE. May I speak?

HOGBIN. **Care — ful...!** (*Pause.*)

SAVAGE. The war was already in you. Do you think hatred has no life? It's born with you. It howls in your first howl. Impatient loathing coiled behind your tongue which on the pretext **rolled out like a python**, a hundred feet of scales... (*Pause.*) The kind man racks his mind how thousands might grapple in the mud for a single woman. The disbelief! Or the lout stab the pensioner's eyes! The kind man should stare down his own throat... (*Pause.*)

SHADE (*in realisation*). Whad' yer mean, this is his home?

FLADDER (*leaping up*). Nobody goes!

SHADE. Fuck that —

FLADDER. **Gendarmes!** (GUMMERY *goes to grab the mirror from* CREUSA.)

SHADE. **My mirror!**

FLADDER. Home the lie, home the sentiment!

SHADE (*grabbing one end of the mirror*). My mirror!

FLADDER. The knife under the pillow, the long, cold marital stare...

EPSOM (*wading in*). **Stuff it, Barry!** (*Gendarmes rush in, pin back* SHADE'S *arms. A breathless pause.*)

FLADDER. Home? What's that? The dead eye of the widow who finds she is no widow? The child's sullen resignation of its place? **Home what's that.** (*Pause.*) Go, if you wish. (*The Gendarmes release him.* SHADE *goes to take the mirror from* GUMMERY.) No Mirror (*He stops.*)

SHADE. No mirror? (*He looks about him.*) **I suffered for that mirror. It's my prize!** (*Pause.*)

FLADDER. The ship goes hooooooooo... (*Pause.*) The ship goes hooooooooo... (*Pause, then* SHADE *dumps to the ground.* GUMMERY *returns the mirror.*)

HELEN. First Troy is under the ashes. Second Troy now. (*She goes to leave.*)

GUMMERY. Second Troy? Of what, lady? Paper?

FLADDER. Paper, yes. Paper Troy now! No more weapons! No more walls! Write everywhere our shame! (HELEN *goes out and* FLADDER *rises.*) **Constitution writers!** (*To* SAVAGE.) How's your spelling?

SAVAGE. Adequate.

FLADDER. Spell agony.

SAVAGE. H — E — L — E

FLADDER. You'll do! (*He sweeps out, followed by* GUMMERY *and* EPSOM. CREUSA *remains, staring at* SAVAGE. *Pause.*)

CREUSA. So there you are...

SAVAGE. Don't start —

CREUSA. There you fucking are —

SAVAGE. **Don't start I said —**

CREUSA. **The Imagination, The Intellect —**

SAVAGE. The rattle of your mundane prejudice and —

CREUSA. **Barmy notions —**

SAVAGE. **Domestic triviality you —**

CREUSA. **Posturing as visions you —**

SAVAGE. **Microscopic obsessionist!**

CREUSA. Snob! (*A pause of exhaustion.*)

SHADE. It's mine, now. (*He indicates* CREUSA *with a nod.*)

SAVAGE. Yes

SHADE. The arse. The cry. The dream. Mine. (*Pause.*)

SAVAGE. Yes. (CREUSA *looks at* SAVAGE, *pitifully.*)

CREUSA. Oh, you mad and forlorn bastard... I couldn't take any more of you! (*Wearily, she takes the mirror and bundle from* SHADE *and goes off.* SHADE *looks a long time into* SAVAGE.)

SHADE. I also have a mind. (SAVAGE *turns to look at him.*)

SAVAGE. You —

SHADE. I also have a mind. (*Pause.*) I don't exhibit it, like a balloon. **The mind.** (*Pause.*) I don't **wag** it.

SAVAGE. No...

SHADE. But it exists. And it has archways, upon archways. And cisterns, and reservoirs also. Fuckall books and fuckall songs but. And anyway, what are those things? They are daggers, also. **Song in the eyes!** (*He feints at* SAVAGE, *and goes off, watched by* HOGBIN.)

HOGBIN (*fearfully*). Get out of 'ere...

SAVAGE. Why?

HOGBIN. This crew. This regiment. 'alf off their 'inges, gates swinging in the 'urricane, **mind yer gob!**

SAVAGE. Why?

HOGBIN. **Mad gates banging!**

SAVAGE. **Go where anyway?** (*Pause.*) Go, he says...the spontaneous retort if things degenerate...nomadic instinct of the urban boy...what are you, a sparrow, off at the first pin drop? A rabbit, pelting at the shadow of the cloud? Nomads have no written culture, you know that...

HOGBIN. Fuck your comprehensiveness...

SAVAGE. **No knowledge on the hoof.**

HOGBIN. Yes, but this — (*Pause.*)

SAVAGE. To go beyond. That's our hunger, that's our thirst. To go beyond, you must stand still. **First paradox of all great journeys.** (*He opens his arms.*) Kiss me, I have told you something.

HOGBIN. You always wanna be kissed —

SAVAGE. **Do it out of gratitude!** (HOGBIN *pecks him.*)

HOGBIN. Who was that, your Mrs who got lost? I think you shoved your cold chisel in 'er cracks and drove a decent woman barmy. Did you? But I think she's kind, as all blasphemers are...

Scene Four

A tumult of paper. Men folding. HOGBIN *on his knees, copying.* HELEN *enters with* A DAUGHTER.

HELEN. **Will whoever brings dead men's ribs and things into my bedroom stop!**

FLADDER (*entering*). Second Troy has paper walls because they offer no defence, and having no defence invite no enemies. All the energies of the inhabitants will be directed towards the examination of our errors. Write reconciliation everywhere, and artists, if there are any, stick pictures on it!

HELEN. It is an offence to tamper with war graves in any case, who is doing it, do you know?

HOGBIN. Not the foggiest...

HELEN. Someone is, I'm not imagining it.

FLADDER. **Where's Savage? Has he made the loving constitution yet?**

HELEN. A bit of thigh, or skull with weird red hair on it? Perhaps the dogs do it?

HOGBIN. Maybe dogs...

HELEN. No shortage of dogs in Second Troy.

HOGBIN. Dogs all over the shop...

HELEN. No, it isn't dogs, it's men. **A corpse in the bed will be next.** (SAVAGE *enters.*)

SAVAGE. The Seven Principles of New Troy.

FLADDER. Seven is it...good...

SAVAGE. The poor will apologize. The rich will forgive. The thief will be compensated. The victim accused.

FLADDER. Of what?

SAVAGE. Tempting the thief.

FLADDER. Good.

SAVAGE. All governors will swim rivers at seventy.

FLADDER. Why?

SAVAGE. To prove their minds are still good.

FLADDER. Yes...

SAVAGE. The sick will dictate morality. The healthy will never be paid.

FLADDER. They have health.

SAVAGE. They have health, yes. The intellectual will be revered until he speaks. The passionate will be in receipt of pension books. (*Pause.*)

FLADDER. That's eight, surely? (SAVAGE *bows.*)

HELEN. When I was fourteen I could tell jokes. And men said, you tell jokes better than a man!

GUMMERY. I don't call that a constitution...

HELEN. But for all their laughing, not one of them would lay a hand on me. Not one!

GUMMERY. Do you, Les?

HELEN. So I stopped telling jokes. And they were all over me! Breaking one another's jaws, and scrapping in the gutter.

GUMMERY (*to* SAVAGE). **I don't call that a constitution.**

HELEN. There is a time for jokes, but it's not now.

SAVAGE (*to* GUMMERY). Nail it to the doors, and all the citizens of Paper Troy will be outraged and stamp their feet, and go around shouting 'Never!' (*Pause.*) Which is good, and the proper condition for a populace to be in.

FLADDER. **Paint it. The seven principles of Paper Troy.**

EPSOM (*to* WORKERS *off*). **Paints!**

GUMMERY (*confused*). Seven? You said eight...

FLADDER. Seven, yes! (*To* SAVAGE.) You see, they gawp at your magnificence... (GUMMERY *stares at the paper.*)

SAVAGE (*patiently, to* GUMMERY). This gives you freedom...

GUMMERY. Freedom?

SAVAGE. To break the stranglehold of the consecutive. You can write seven twice. Or not number them at all.

GUMMERY (*shaking his head*). Confusing...

SAVAGE. Yes!

GAY. My mother called me Gay. Do you know why? I don't know why, I'm sure. And I had a sister called FELICITY. What was that about? Felicity died, naturally, and of such a painful illness! But I am going to be gay. I am. (HELEN *leans fondly over her daughter.*) **Don't touch me with those gnawed and kneaded tits.** (*Pause. She smiles, kissing her mother fondly.*)

SAVAGE. Knowledge is a suite of rooms. Dirty rooms, unswept as museums in the provinces. And to enter each room you must leave with the woman at the door some priceless thing, which feels part of yourself and your identity, so that it feels like ripping skin. And the keepers sit in piles of discarded treasures, like the pelts of love or children's pity, and at each successive door the piles are less because few stagger such long distances, until there comes a door at which there lies a small, white rag stained as a dishcloth, which may be sanity **And if you think that is the end you are mistaken, it is the beginning.** (*Pause.*) And people say, 'I know myself'. Have you heard that? Never! they know the contents of one room. (*Pause.*)

FLADDER. But who'd want knowledge if knowledge meant I could simply look at her, and looking see only a hundred pounds of flesh, which by virtue of its shape defines her beautiful? If knowledge is to be so cool I'd say stuff knowledge **what do you find Helen, Dr Savage? She made me think appalling thought.** (*Pause.*) Lay down for my inspection every inch of your infatuation. (*Pause.*) What, no words, and you a teacher? (*Pause.*) You see, if she is not impossible to see without she wrecks our peace, what did we suffer for? **Imagine the temper in the war cemeteries!** (*Pause.*)

SAVAGE. All my life I have searched out Helen of Troy. And if you stuck a bin of offal there and called it Helen, I should have to stoop to it. (*The fraction of a pause.*)

FLADDER. Bin! (*He goes out.*)

SHADE (*calling off*). **A bin!**

HELEN. Oh, doctor, they will chain you to it and you will suffocate on stench for uttering one solid truth upon another... (*A bin is manoeuvered on.*)

CREUSA (*entering*). Oh God, what has he done?

HOGBIN. Been a silly bugger all over again — (THE SOLDIERS *chain him to the bin by his wrists.* GAY *sits down on the floor.*)

GAY. The amount of killing I have seen! My father, for example, on the floor and skinned. Paris! Yes, it's true! They skinned him. And my grandfather was **inside out.** I have seen the lot, I can assure you, and I thought to myself, Gay, they want you to go **insane.** So I decided there and then I would not. **I declined to be insane.** (*Pause.*) I think Paper Troy won't last. And then what? Another pile of murders and a skinning or two! (*Pause.*) My mother gave birth to me with my father's thing in her gob **I just know it.** He took his clothes off while she contracted and lay beside her. **I just know he did they were like that**. So I've seen the lot, really, and am I insane? **Quite the contrary.** (*She skips out.*)

HOGBIN (*a crablike move to* SAVAGE). Too fucking clever —

SAVAGE. Away you skinny newt —

HOGBIN. Night's coming in and storm clouds full of freezing rain —

SAVAGE. You book-snapping terrier —

HOGBIN. You will perish of exposure you unhealthy sod of fat —

SAVAGE. You whimpering abortion of a greyhound's toss —

HOGBIN. **Now, then, truth-teller!** (*He rolls about the floor.*) No chains! (*He somersaults.*) No bin! (*He goes towards* CREUSA, *who has drawn a paper over herself. A storm rumbles.* HOGBIN *gets under with her. He pokes out his head.*) Adopt the nature of the chameleon. (*He withdraws. A ragged book flies out. Then* HOGBIN'S *head.*) Borkman and Salberstein. (*He goes back in.*)

SAVAGE. Oh, rain on, oh, dark on, and gales roar up the beach like bombers levelling the streets. I know what Helen is, I know what Helen is! Another shell in the boiling breech! Oh, to be at sieges, at every siege that ever was, and throw in death from hills, the breakfast goes, the kitchen goes, the crockery went up a hundred feet, the horse stood at the traffics lights and then down came its parted hooves, one in the garden of the spinster, one in the orphanage. I trawl, I dig, I excavate! Under your half-truths! The lecturer's voice is a whip, the vicar's lectern is a rack for thrashing youth! Who trusts the smiles on the library steps? Razor blades in the dictionary! I know! I know what Helen is! She's all that's unforgivable! (FLADDER *enters in an overcoat. He sits.*)

FLADDER. I like the night. I feel what in the day I must deny has every right to full consideration. Say you understand me. (*He looks at the paper tent.*) What is going on in the paper house?

SAVAGE. My student is struck dumb by the body of my wife and theoryless for once, explores her with his tongue. And she's another man's thing, by which he risks castration at the least. A real cocktail of pleasures, but you'd appreciate it, what's love without the risk of death?

FLADDER (*implacably*). I wish to be tried, and if necessary, executed. (*Pause.*)

SAVAGE (*astutely*). On no charge, presumably?

FLADDER. No charges.

SAVAGE. And the verdict?

FLADDER. Guilty. And I prosecute myself.

SAVAGE. So new Troy opens with the execution of the governor?

FLADDER. I'll demand the ultimate penalty.

SAVAGE. And I'll grant it. I take it I'm the magistrate?

FLADDER. Who else? Are you not the only criminal? (*He goes out.*)

SAVAGE. If every man is ashamed, and you are not ashamed. If every man is guilty, and you refuse guilt...**What then!**

CREUSA (*emerging, adjusting her clothing*). He says...(*A small, dry laugh.*) He says...I drive all anger from his mind...he says...listen to this...to see me naked kills ambition...the peace, the peace, he says...

SAVAGE. Listen, I have —

CREUSA. **No, you listen.** (*Pause.*) He says incredible things no man ever said of me. But he's impotent as yet. **Understandable!** If you put such store by one woman, to come erect at once would be no compliment, would it? I'm honoured by his crisis. (*She looks at herself, bemused.*) I've been through hell, but you were hell as well...what happened to our son? (*Pause.*) Oh, look, I ask as casually as one might for a book or newspaper! I had all the instincts but I learned to suffocate them in a bag, I don't threaten you with maternal rages, so where did he, you can tell...(*Pause.*)

SAVAGE. He. (*Pause.*)

CREUSA. It's me who broke the bond, and watched the three of you stagger out of my life, no claims and no reproaches, what's a child in any case, we stepped across whole ditchfuls, I remember...(*Pause.*)

SAVAGE. He. (*Pause.*)

CREUSA. The product of a joyless copulation, no I have no temper, boot the sentiment, boot the mother stuff, **He what.** (*Pause.*)

SAVAGE. Whatever you imagine is as likely as the truth. As painful, or as painless.

CREUSA. Still, I want to know, however futile —

SAVAGE. Dream it instead —

CREUSA. I do, I dream it often but —

SAVAGE. **What difference does it make.**

CREUSA. **It makes a difference!** (*Pause.*) Tell me, and I'll swallow it. Down, like a single pill, gollop, and gone! Life continues, under Hogbin's fascinated stare or beaten by the Greeks, today it's rheumatism, tomorrow, plague, the sticky belt of crisis but first what happened to my son? (*Pause.*) The mundane bit of life I mundanely delivered... (*Pause.*)

SAVAGE. I don't know. I lost him. (*Pause.*)

CREUSA. Lost him...

SAVAGE. Lost him, yes...

CREUSA. Mislaid him...

SAVAGE. Mislaid him, yes, no, I lost him.

CREUSA. Lost him?

SAVAGE. **Lost, you know the word, it happened all over Europe.** Drifting infants, in dead men's uniforms...

CREUSA. You —

SAVAGE. **Lost my child and helped my father die!**

CREUSA. Oh, you —

SAVAGE. And not guilty!

CREUSA. You —

SAVAGE. **Not guilty, no!** (*She stares at him. Pause.*)

CREUSA. Hold my hand, you terrible mouth, biting the concrete, your gums all shredded and your lips all torn...terrible mouth on you... (*She holds his hands.* HOGBIN *emerges and looks. To* HOGBIN, *not turning.*) It's all right...these are old bruises we have to bruise again... (*She gets up, goes out.*)

HOGBIN. Funny, ain't it, any bastard can serve a woman properly but me. Any phlegm-stained criminal to do a violation of a child is rigid as a tree branch. Any dancing mannikin dribbling on a deb gets seven inches on request. **What about me!**

SAVAGE. Patience...

HOGBIN. **Patience...!**

SAVAGE. She is. (*Pause.*) It's only a space.

HOGBIN. A space?

SAVAGE. A mobile space.

HOGBIN. **A mobile space?**

SAVAGE. You think by parroting you diminish truth you hate to entertain —

HOGBIN. **It's oblivion!** (*Pause.*)

SAVAGE. So's a grave. A space enclosing oblivion. (*Pause.*)

HOGBIN. Want it anyway. So did you, once... (HELEN *enters, holding a fragment.*)

HELEN. Neck bone. (*She lifts the lid of* SAVAGE'S *bin, drops it in, replacing the lid.*) I think they do this because they desire me. I may be

wrong. It could be hatred, but then, what's hatred? I think it's desire also,
what do you say? (*She looks at* HOGBIN.)

HOGBIN (*cautiously*.) I wouldn't disagree with you —

HELEN. Oh listen, I am sad tonight, so stuff your tact. I want a conversation.

HOGBIN. Stuff it, yes...

HELEN. I get no sleep. I go to my room, and even as I go towards the door
I think to myself, oh, the futility of this...

HOGBIN. Know the feeling...

HELEN. I fling the sheet aside and there — **Why do you always agree with
me?** (*Pause.* HOGBIN *shrugs*.) I fling the sheet back and — (*Pause.*) Of
course I suffer all the consequences. More lined. And more bad
tempered. The face becomes a landscape of insomnia and yet the overall
effect is I am **more desirable.** Yes! It's true! Do you think I am insane? Do
you think, poor thing, she is deluded? There is no point in the conversation if you hold that opinion, none at all, no, I tell you the truth because
you are unhappy, I ditched modesty decades ago and so would you, I have
had nine children, my belly's a pit, or as the poetically-inclined say when
they're lapping me, a sandy strand from which the tide receded leaving
feathered frontiers. Ugly, but who's deterred? You see, for compliments
I have a perfect memory...(*Pause.*) This is not a conversation, is it? I am
doing all the talking. (EPSOM *and* GUMMERY *rush in with* FLADDER
between them, stripped and beaten.)

FLADDER. I am the murderer! I am the victim!

HELEN (*horrified*). **What have you done to him!**

FLADDER. I am the killer! **Hangman in attendance, please!**

HELEN. **What have you done to his face!**

GUMMERY. He told me to!

FLADDER (*to* SAVAGE). **Sentence me, then!**

HELEN. His face, look...

GUMMERY. **He told me to...!**

FLADDER. Innocent squaddies! (*She goes to wipe away the blood.*) **Don't
touch the assassin's face!** (*She stands back.*) I asked them to hurt me, and
all they could think of was their fists, what other tortures do they know
about? Love? **No chair for the accused**, I kneel, no, that's too comfortable, I squat, what was the sentence, death?

SAVAGE. Yes...

FLADDER. Didn't hear it.

SAVAGE. It goes without saying...

FLADDER. **Cacophony in court!** Listen, the destruction of cities, the
wrecking of fleets, the burning of crops, infanticide by numbers, all this
is so much **trivia**. War crimes, rubbish, no. In Paper Troy the only crimes
are crimes against the self.

HELEN. I think you are the most insatiable exhibitionist.

FLADDER (*glaring at her*). Exhibitionism you would know about, who
hung your cunt out to all youth, **I've seen her do it like the butcher
showing meat.**

HELEN. Get up and wash your face, will you...?

FLADDER. What we do to others is no sin, it's self-murder I prosecute, the only crimes are crimes against the self, that's the source of cruelty!

HELEN. Wash your face, please...

FLADDER. Wash it, why? Wash yours, it's black with terror. **You think to show your arse is revelation?** (*She slaps him. Pause.*)

HELEN. You see, you bring out the worst in everyone. (*Pause.* FLADDER *hangs his head.*)

GUMMERY. He was such a bugger once, a proper head-hacker, I saw him swallow blood hot from the severed arteries, the head still rolling in the fosse...

HELEN. Terrible decline... It comes from having Helen back...

SAVAGE (*briskly*). No executioner. Pity. Paper gaol, then, until such time as paper death sets in.

FLADDER (*seeing* SHADE *enter*). **Here's the man to do it.** (*They look at* SHADE.)

EPSOM. Go 'ome now, Barry, if yer wish. And take the mirror. (*Pause.*)

SHADE. Home? What's that?

FLADDER. In him, even, whose mouth is a brass purse of pain, some rotted quality of personal perfection must persist, all gnawed and spoiled by terror and abuse, **deep though!** (*Suddenly,* SHADE *flies at him.*)

HOGBIN (*horrified*). Hey...!

SAVAGE (*looking*). Not looking...

HOGBIN. Oi, you're the —

SAVAGE. **Not looking** —

HOGBIN. **Magistrate!**

HELEN (*as* SHADE *works on* FLADDER).
His little sob at coming
His great shout at coming
His little spilling
His great splash of fluid
His snivelling at betrayal
His great cataclysms of despair
His skittering with infants
His flinging of the baby at the wall
What could you make of that brute and boy (*Pause.*)
No man made me more eager to betray him or more willing to come back... (*Pause.*)

HOGBIN. He ain't dead... (*Pause.*)

HELEN. Not dead? (*She laughs, as* SHADE *walks away from the kneeling* FLADDER.)

SHADE. The worst thing that can happen to a compulsive apologist I think, is to lose his tongue...

HELEN. Lose his...

SHADE. Finish Paper Troy.

HELEN. His tongue...

SHADE (*tossing it away*). And paper knives —

HELEN. **No tongue** —

SHADE (*holding a vile thing*). I had to rip it by its roots. **No private life in New Troy! No clamour of apology!** (*Pause.*)

HELEN. Put it back...

SHADE (*turning to her*). Put it back? Why, did it please you very much, lapping your sour flavours? (EPSOM *laughs*.) **No more of that either.** He only watches now, his eyeballs do the talking.

HELEN. Put it back...

SHADE (*thrusting it at her*). You.

HELEN. The voice. The words. Are what desire is. The message is arousal. Or we're cattle. You have castrated him.

SHADE. No, I left those shrivelled things intact.

HELEN. **You have castrated him.** (*Pause.*) He could mutter me into upheavals no shoving hip could copy, earthquakes by his bawdy —

EPSOM. **Lend us the tongue, then!**

HELEN. Oh, you sham male, dog on its hind legs dancing —

EPSOM. **Lend us it!**

HELEN. Parody of masculinity —

SHADE (*flinging the tongue to* EPSOM). Bury it, with honours, since it commanded us at epic slaughters, or pickle it for youth to gawp at. And this fat one, let him record its wit from recollections, in eight volumes. As for this bitch, new queen now, for new Troy. Where's my looted woman?

CREUSA. No thank you.

SHADE. New Queen I said. (*To* HELEN.) And you, her slut. (*He goes to the kneeling figure of* FLADDER, *puts his hands on* FLADDER'S *shoulders, embraces him.*) Don't think cruel men have not also suffered, or victims spluttered terrible savagery in tears... (*Pause.*) I'm looking for a god. (*Pause He turns to* SAVAGE.) Could it be you?

Scene Five

A Beach. GAY, *with a stick.* A BOY, *seated.*

GAY. Reasons for the fall of Paper Troy. One! (THE BOY *hesitates*.) Come on, oh, do come on, or I will beat you!

BOY. Erm...

GAY. One! The degeneracy of the aristocracy and their flirtation with the arts. Two! The martial ardour of the warriors could find no satisfaction in origami! Three! Are you listening, I don't think you try at all, this is **History** I'm teaching you! And stop fidgetting, or I will beat you! (*Exasperated pause.*) I sometimes think, people are such swine, such inveterate swine. And then I think, no, you can make them better.

BOY. By beating them?

GAY. By beating them, yes! How else? (*She sees a figure, off.*) Oh, no, here comes that horrid old man again! Don't encourage him. Because he's blind we all go silly, he knows that, he uses that to exploit us. (HOMER *enters, blind.*) **You are not to put your hand into my dress again.** (*He* *stops.*) I think the beach should be a place for children to be children and not poked about by peculiar old men.

HOMER. You are not a child.

GAY. I am a child. I am thirteen. Obviously I am a child.

HOMER. You are not a child, and I am not an old man.

GAY. Conundrum.

BOY. What?

GAY. Conundrum. He says all these things, these conundrums and things, and the next thing you know —

HOMER. Stop —

GAY. Hand up your —

HOMER. **Stop.** (*She concedes.*) I am not an old man because I know nothing. And you are not a child because you know it all. Now give me your hand. (*She extends it.* HOMER *draws it quickly to his crutch.*)

GAY. There! I knew that would happen!

HOMER. **A god lives there.**

HELEN (*entering*). The author of the Iliad.

GAY. He is trying to make me insane...

HELEN. The author of the Odyssey.

GAY. **He is trying to make me insane!** (*She pulls away, runs off.*)

HOMER. The young...! No charity! So cruel, which is their fascination...

BOY. She beats me with a twig!

HOMER. Lucky fellow...

BOY. Right round the face sometimes, whip! Because I don't know ten reasons for the fall of Paper Troy.

HOMER. There are not ten reasons.

BOY. That's what I say! (*He hurries off.*)

HELEN. I hate your songs. Do you mind this? The ripping livers and the splash of brains. The prosody is marvellous but. I must say this and fuck the consequences. The torrents of intestine and the ravens picking skulls **I also am so violent**, were you always blind? When their attacks were beaten off we maimed the wounded. With kitchen knives, me and the Trojan women, hacked them in the ditch, trimming the features off their heads like turnips for the market and their cocks we cropped **Don't say you never heard of this** were you born blind or was it horror spread some merciful film across your retina, and what's pity, I do think pity is no substitute for truth —

HOMER. Helen —

HELEN. **I refuse to clap your songs.** (*Pause.*) I loved Troy, because Troy was to sin. Why did you never say that? But him who took me there was not a sinner, only an exhibitionist, and not my equal. **Don't you know the hell it is to find no man your equal?** Say that, in your next book. That was the agony of Troy, not slippery swords or old men massacred, but Helen's awful loneliness in dream...

HOMER. Helen...

HELEN. Do what you like with my daughter — when history gets to a child no mother can be of the least relief.

HOMER (*holding out his arms*). Helen! (*He encloses her. She weeps.*
SAVAGE *appears with* HOGBIN *pushing the bin.*)

SAVAGE. I said, if I am the god, why do I have to drag the bin? Put wheels
on it, he said...

HELEN (*pulling free of* HOMER). What are you?

SAVAGE. What am I?

HELEN. You come here, first a clerk and now a god — it's obvious you want
to destroy me —

SAVAGE. Me —

HELEN. **What else are you here for!**

HOGBIN (*demonstratively*). The Interlude of the Bin! Within the bin —
(*He removes the lid.*) The fruits of the hospital! I construct — I
demonstrate — the vital elements of the Suffering Biped — **One!** (*He
reaches into the offal.*) It's a — (*He looks at a shapeless thing.*) Call it a
foot — (*He places it on the ground.*) This transports the lie around — the
biped is manoeuverable, it is not still, no, it stamps in unison, the foot
being also for **dancing**, a futile repetition aimed at creating social unity,
Another lie and also, **kicking**, the ecstasy experienced by the biped in
inflicting pain, **Two!** (*He dips in again.*) The knee! (*He looks at a
shapeless thing.*) Call it a knee —

SAVAGE (*staring at* HOMER). Listen —

HOGBIN. Why not a knee —

SAVAGE. Listen, will you?

HOGBIN (*laying the piece down*). I'm talking —

SAVAGE. This is him who —

HOGBIN. **I'm talking, aren't I?** (*Pause.*) Knee. For kneeling with. To
imaginary forces such as God, or actual forces such as the party, the
murderer, etcetera, a complex joint enabling the biped to grovel most
convincingly —

SAVAGE. **Ho — mer!** (*He throws himself at* HOMER'S *feet and kisses the
hem of his garment.*)

HOGBIN. Also, for driving into softer organs such as the stomach or the
genitals, to render ineffective the thing I number **Three** — (*He dips in
again at random.*) The organ of increase! (*He pulls out a shapeless thing.*)
Call it a dick — why not a dick — and with the other bit — two elements
with which... (*he stares at the thing*) the biped...in an extravaganza of
futility...pretends to...shake off consciousness...or fails to...**Ribs!** (*He
reaches in, stops in mid-movement. To* SAVAGE.) You mustn't do
that...he may be the very wickedest of bastards...

SAVAGE. **The great man lends us hope...**

HOGBIN. You say that because you sense you are a great man yourself, but
undiscovered...

SAVAGE (*to* HOMER). We squabble, my student and I, my desperate and
sadistic student, we — but you would know, you with your flocks of
followers —

HOGBIN. Creeping...

SAVAGE. Clustering around you for the least perception which —

HOGBIN. Creeping...

SAVAGE. **Let me worship somebody!** (*Pause.*) So barren, isn't it, a life without prostration? (*To* HOGBIN.) **And that goes for all juvenile iconoclasts!** (*Pause. To* HOMER.) Savage, PhD, lecturer in classics, theses on metre and the first six books... (*Pause.*) Beloved genius...I call you genius...though he would say there's no such thing...**There is and this is it**... (*Pause.*)Speak to me...a little philosophical deduction...no, that's a lot to ask, a real impertinence, forgive me...anything would do... (*Pause.*) Not anything, that's silly, not anything, not the time of day, no, but a little distillation? Or is distillation now impossible? (*Pause.*) **Come on, I wrote two books about you!**

HOGBIN. Ribs! (*He pulls a shapeless thing from the bin.*) Call it ribs, all right? (*He places it down.*) In the shelter of which the biped hides his **heart**, formerly conceived as organ of feeling, passion, etcetera, but now exposed as leathery and boring **pump**.

HOMER. I hate the young. When I was young even, I hated the young...(*Pause.*)

SAVAGE (*to* HOMER). You are the greatest poet in the world. Of any time. Of any culture. (*Pause.*) I wonder if you heard? I said —

HOMER. You imagine you compliment me.

SAVAGE. Don't I?

HOMER. And having complimented me, you expect the compliment to give me pleasure.

SAVAGE. Doesn't it? (*Pause. Suddenly, shockingly,* HELEN *leaps on* HOGBIN *and wrestles him.*)

HOGBIN. Oi! (HELEN *and* HOGBIN *roll about. She bears him down.*) Oi! (*She laughs with delight.*) Oi! (*They roll over the floor.*)

HOMER. The great artist drifts beyond the common consciousness, like a child carried to sea by a raft. The beach gets further, the paddlers get further, the weak swimmers, then the strong swimmers, all out of reach, until — **You are writing it down!**

SAVAGE. No, I —

HOMER. **Liar. Heard the pen.**

SAVAGE (*innocently*). Was I?

HELEN (*to* HOGBIN, *climbing off him*). Be my lover.

HOGBIN. No!

HELEN. They say no now! Listen! No, he says. Look, I plead...!

HOGBIN. Don't wanna...

HELEN. We will have a child and call it — (*To* HOMER.) **Don't look at me like that I am not infertile.** (HOGBIN *scrambles to his feet.*)

HELEN. Listen...! (*She cups her ear.*) The daily chant of Laughing Troy...

SHADE (*entering*). The word. (*He looks at them.*)
    The word today is Us.
    All say it.
    Us.
    It soothes the soul, it calms the temper, can't hear you.
    Us. (HOMER *starts to leave.*)
    I thought you were blind, not dumb. (*He stops.*) I also have a mind.

HOMER. Us.

SHADE. Excellent. I think with vast and bloated genius, to stoop is healthy. (*He turns to the others.*) Everybody!

ALL. Us. (*Pause. He turns to leave.*)

SAVAGE. Excuse me, am I still a god?

SHADE. Why not? Aren't you still ugly? (*He goes to leave again.*)

SAVAGE. Tomorrow's word then! (SHADE *stops.*) If you're looking for suggestions... (*Pause.*) **Must.**

SHADE. Must...?

SAVAGE. **Us** and **Must.** The twin pillars of history... (SHADE *goes out. Pause. They look at* SAVAGE *critically.*) I did not come here to sit on a beach... (*They stare at him.*) Where's knowledge? Where does it lie? In meditation? The lillies and the rhyming couplets? The whispering sandal in the aromatic garden? **No poet ever told us anything.** (HOGBIN *looks at* HOMER .) And why? **Because he never governed.** That's why he's blind, he only looks inside. **All right Mr Homer you can abuse me now.** (*Pause.*) I'm waiting, in a lather of submission... (*Pause.*)

HELEN. You are not a very great man, Dr Savage...

SAVAGE. His lashing, please...

HELEN. Or even very dignified...

SAVAGE. His lashing, not yours...! (*Pause, then* HOMER *goes off.*) I am beneath contempt...

HELEN. Yes, but he's looking for my daughter. (*She turns to go, stops, looks at* HOGBIN, *who is replacing the offal in the bin.*) What's the matter, do you love another woman? (HOGBIN *shrugs.*) I hope I shan't hate you. I'm such a hater. It's the burden of my life.

HOGBIN. I'm sorry, I —

HELEN. Don't! (*Pause. To* SAVAGE.) He was going to apologize! Or is that right? Perhaps he knows, if he really tried, he could love me? (*She goes out.* MACLUBY *appears.*)

MACLUBY. The Pruning of Helen. (SAVAGE *and* HOGBIN *fill the bin, replace the lid.*) The pruning of Helen may have been — this is the nature of political decisions — spontaneous. A flash of intuition or a stab of malice, **What do you think History is, deliberation?** On the other hand it may have been the outcome of long and acrimonious debate within the ruling circle, **What do you think History is, spasms?** (*To* SAVAGE, *who is going out.*) Oi! (SAVAGE *stops.*) He also sins who only writes the words. But you know that. (MACLUBY *goes out.* CREUSA *enters.*)

CREUSA. Slave one day. Queen the next. Would you believe? The transformations! But happy by order, and to be illiterate. Difficult, when I was not illiterate in the first place. This Troy to be in single syllables. Difficult. Or hard, should say. (*She exerts her imagination.*) **My — plain — face — to — be — the — badge — of — Troy.** Done it! (*She tries again.*) **And — in — my — life — the — crowd — will — see — and — love — its — self — not — stoop — to — snobs — nor — lick — the — arse — of — beauty — Beauty's two...** (*Pause.*) Shade's Troy. (*She parrots.*) I also have a mind...! (*Pause. She looks at* HOGBIN.) Will you talk to me, I have given up all hope of a quiet life, and a quiet life when I had it I despised, it was not quiet, it was clay, it was not quiet, it was mud, quiet is something else, not dense but light I think. I left notes for you in so many places, my scrambling love, my rodent, I was burrowed, I was tunnelled, all my dark exposed to daylight, a tent uptipped, a parcel with your fingers at the strings, the haste, the impatience, the breathless hunt, and your great wail of desperation, did you get my notes, every tree trunk I left letters in and every litterbin, no, I exaggerate, some I did pass by, do I embarrass you at all, you look so, I am so rarely this enthusiastic and you look, **oh, fuck I have offended him,** calm down, calm down, there I'm calm now, I am so glad to see you, there, statement of extreme reserve, **don't you want to fuck now,** shh! I could, almost, I could, yes, I could almost **beat you, I also have a mind,** please speak or don't I leave you room, I don't, do I, here's room. (*She stops. Pause.*)

HOGBIN. Cold today... (*Pause.*)

CREUSA. Cold today. You? Ah. Shh! Could let out such a torrent. Could let out such a volley but no, shh. I have done everything. I have been everythinged, and you, a balding and precocious youth can **Who's impotent at that** for which no criticism can make me who has done everything and been everythinged — (*Pause.*) If I believed in gods I'd say some godlike bugger had sprinkled me with what — delirium — to entertain himself — cold, is it? All right, just sit, to sit with you would be enough, and say a few words, or nothing if you — (*He sits.*) Thank you. (*Pause.*) I thank him. (*Pause.*)

HOGBIN. Cold today...

CREUSA. We are like that. We are! We are so inconsistent. We are liars without meaning it. And now I'm cold as well. Excellently cold. Excellently off the idea. Excellent. I could no more have you than. I am to speak in words of single syllables I must remind you. It is the function of my majesty. (*Pause.*) Arse is one syllable. Cunt obviously. It is a miracle when two moods coincide. It is a sacrament. **Three syllables!** (*A long pause, then she lets out a cry.*) Oh, God... (*Pause.*) Oh, God, you have met someone else... (*Pause.*)

Scene Six

The Government. EPSOM *carries on the mirror.*

SHADE. Gather round me. Come on, gather round me, comrades in arms, etcetera, treaders of the bowel carpet and the brain mat — (*He opens his arms to them. He clutches them round the shoulders. They stare into the mirror.*) Oh, we are ageing! Oh, we are shedding! Look, the ploughed up skins, we are hanging off our cheek bones and our eyes are dim. Look deep, look deep, we slew arbitrarily and we pitied arbitrarily. Look deep. Speech, Les.

EPSOM. Speech?

SHADE. Speech! Yes! This is the frame of greatness, did you think battle was your forte? Never, battle's for the bullock this is where proper violence belongs. **Words!** Les!

EPSOM. Can't —

SHADE. He can't, he can't, Brian, you —

GUMMERY. Must I?

SHADE. You must, old friend.

GUMMERY. Look at yourself then, Barry —

SHADE. Brian, I do —

GUMMERY. Look 'ard and tell us, is it a healthy face is looking back at you?

SHADE. Not healthy, no —

GUMMERY. Or noble?

SHADE. Noble, no —

GUMMERY. Regard the beak, the way the eyes protrude —

SHADE. They do, and I forgive your rudeness —

EPSOM. Yellow skin —

SHADE. Thank you —

EPSOM. And puffy round yer lids —

SHADE. Oh, Les, you have discovered speech —

GUMMERY. Is there pity in the eyeball?

SHADE. Pity? None —

GUMMERY. Mercy?

SHADE. Mercy? **Keep the mirror still** we're looking for my — what —

GUMMERY. Mercy —

SHADE. No, can't see it, Brian, unless that bloodshot vein is it... I think sometimes, they want me to be cruel. They bay at cruelty, but still I think they want me to be cruel. I think even the beaten man wants to be beaten. Why is that?

SAVAGE (*entering*). The governor is the nightmare of the populace... (*Pause.*)

SHADE. Leave me with the doctor. We must define new life, the gutters and the ceilings of New Troy. How laughter might be made as sharp as wire, and dancing a new drill...(GUMMERY *and* EPSOM *leave.* SHADE *looks into* SAVAGE. *Pause.*) **Supposing we trusted one another!** (*Silence.*) Supposing. (*Pause.*) Just supposing. (*Pause.*) I use the word trust loosely. Because I imagine there is trust and trust. Trust I think I fathom, but **Trust...!** What's that? (*Pause.* GUMMERY *comes back in.* SHADE *detects him in the mirror with alarm.*) **Don't return without warning me!** (GUMMERY *freezes.*) What is it, Brian, you made me jump.

GUMMERY. Old Helen of Old Troy

SHADE. What about her?

GUMMERY. Is carrying 'er 'usband round the 'ouse on 'er back. 'e croaks on 'er like a sun-burned frog. Down alleys and through the estates. And 'is saliva everywhere, buckets of, the tongueless dribble, it appears, in excess, and it's making puddles where women exercise their dogs...

SHADE. All right...

GUMMERY. This was the cause of ten years' bleeding and now look at 'er, bare legs and filthy black — It makes a pig of everyone who raged for ten years at the gates if she's to be a slut with unwashed legs —

SHADE. I can see you're anxious —

GUMMERY. History, Barry!

SHADE. History, yes, but even Helen ages —

GUMMERY. Quicker than most, but dignity would help. (*He goes out.*)

SHADE. I take his point. And once they sold her piss in little bottles. Well, so it was said by servants who crossed to our lines with buckets of the stuff. Could have been the cat's for all we knew. One piss is just like any other. (*Pause.*) Or isn't it?

SAVAGE. No.

SHADE. Some smeared their wounds with it. Some swallowed it with cordials. The very depth of barminess. Or was it?

SAVAGE. No. (*Pause.*)

SHADE. What do you want, Doctor Savage?

SAVAGE. Knowledge.

SHADE. How?

SAVAGE. Through you.

SHADE. Through me? But aren't I coarse and stupid?

SAVAGE. Yes. But stupidity's my instrument.

SHADE (*smiles*). It's night, I let all insults fly, like vermin coming through the floorboards **rat on the gob!**

SAVAGE. You hate all kisses which aren't quick —

SHADE. Yes, I admit it.

SAVAGE. And whispers of impossible intentions —

SHADE. I admit that too! Night's the time for filth and for confessions! **Loathsome insect in the sink!** You think I will like you if you abuse me. Intellectual's privilege? (*He goes to* SAVAGE, *close.*) I think my whim, my unrestrained and brutal impulse, spewed from the depths of my defective character and made by you into the monosyllables of late Trojan law, would in their essence be no worse than all the caring calculations of fifty trembling humanists, do you agree or not? (*Pause.*)

SAVAGE. Reserve my judgement.

SHADE. Reserve your judgement — (*He sees* EPSOM *in the mirror.*) **What is it Les yer made me jump!** (EPSOM *enters.*) Still up, old son? What is it, indigestion?

EPSOM. She's placed these adverts. (*He holds out some postcards.*)

SHADE. Must I look?

EPSOM. In corner shops.

SHADE. Must I? You read. (*He goes to the window.*) Look, the very paring of a moon, a nail of moon, against the plague pit of the sky, the word tonight is **Hack.** You could hack pods of pregnancy with the moon's hook...

EPSOM (*reading*). Helen, formerly of Troy —

SHADE. Don't you love moons, doctor? They teach us all is shit, by shining on the good and bad alike...

EPSOM. Model, seeks interesting work part-time —

SHADE. **Stop that!**

EPSOM (*stops reading*). I mean, if she's no better than a whore — then what did we — ten years of — (*Pause.*)

SHADE. She was a whore! Why else did we go there? I think the sex thing is such a punishment to us. I think you cattle. Don't you? Copulating cattle? Seeing the rear of a cow I think, its hips are not unlike a stooping tart, and us likewise no doubt, our bits droop like a dog's. **Human dignity what's that.**

SAVAGE. I don't know.

SHADE. Don't you?

SAVAGE. I think it's love.

SHADE. What love? You chuck words up like a dead men's ashes, what love? The love of criminals in cars or bankrupt marriages. **What?**

SAVAGE. I don't know! I'm frightened to know!

SHADE. The love of old men for their benches, what!

SAVAGE. **I'm frightened to know!**

SHADE. Stare in the glass! (*He fetches the mirror.*) Stare in the glass.

SAVAGE (*on his knees still*). I don't like mirrors...

SHADE. No one does. (*He places it close to* SAVAGE.)

SAVAGE. Avoided mirrors all my life —

SHADE. Because you're ugly —

SAVAGE. Am I? Yes I —

SHADE. Ugly, yes, go on —

SAVAGE. Shaved without one, you can see —

SHADE. Go on —

SAVAGE. Lots of hairs get missed, my wife, she used to say you are the most ungroomed and unprepossessing man I ever — do you think it honours you to be dishevelled — I shun fashion like a —

SHADE. Digressing, doctor —

SAVAGE. As if for some reason there was sin in elegance.

SHADE. Digression on digression —

SAVAGE. I do find speaking to a mirror very —

SHADE. Now your eyes are shut —

SAVAGE. Are they — my eyes —

SHADE. Shut, yes —

SAVAGE. **I think if love lies anywhere it's on the other side of shame.** (*Pause.*)

CREUSA (*who has entered*). Don't believe him, will you? His confessions? The routine torrent of his preposterous sins... (SAVAGE *looks at her, very long.*)

SAVAGE (*pause*). This — vilifying hag — obsessed me with her fundament. The breath turned lead, went solid in my lung, to see her knicker on the stair...I have to say this, she moved me to oaths and superlatives, so I won't speak. Knowledge compels stillness.

SHADE. This private life! I do shudder. This stew of knotted flesh! I do writhe. (*Pause. He turns to* SAVAGE.) How can we make the new man? (*Pause.*) I think he must live in the street. In public always, where nothing uncommon can be done. Can you do this?

SAVAGE. Yes...

SHADE. Laughing. Dancing. I think he should move and think in crowds. Can you write this?

SAVAGE. Yes...

SHADE. Once, when I saw men with miserable faces, staring at the ground, I nutted them. In streets in Attica where I ran yobbish prior to the war I said cheer up you cunt and if they did not grin to order rammed my forehead through their gristle. This was instinct but now I see it also must be politics. (*Pause.*) New Troy. The land of laughter... (*Pause. He looks to* SAVAGE.) Write it, then...

CREUSA. And Helen? (*They look at her.*) Helen who is all clandestine fuck? (*Pause.*)

SHADE. I see no place for Helen, do you, Dr Savage? No place for her in Laughing Troy? Her ego and her filthy legs? Her mouth and acts of endless privacy? She is all I and this is the age of we...

SAVAGE. I has no arms. (*Pause. He looks up, half-curious.*) Does it? The letter? (*Pause.*) I is a single stem? (*Pause.*)

CREUSA (*with rising horror*). Oh, God, he's —

SHADE (*to* SAVAGE). Go on. More cogitation. Further elaboration of the infant thought...

CREUSA. Listen —

SHADE. **I think because I have to.**

SHADE. Oh, yes, you do, you do.

SAVAGE. **And having thought it — out thought! Vile object, out for scrutiny!** (*Pause.*) Helen, who has grown so wild, Helen might be — (*He struggles.*)

CREUSA. Listen, I said —

SHADE. **Shut up, you.** (*Pause. He goes to* SAVAGE.) Won't help the thought to birth. You birth it, you conceived ...

SAVAGE. Yes...

SHADE. **Terrible labour of the thought!**

SAVAGE. Pruned... (*Pause.*)

SHADE. Pruned? (*Pause. He walks up and down. Suddenly* SAVAGE *lets out a terrible cry.*)

SAVAGE. **Knowledge!** (SHADE *hurries out, bundling* CREUSA *with him.* SAVAGE *rocks on his knees.* MACLUBY *appears.*)

MACLUBY. Knowledge...(SAVAGE *turns, sees him. He scrambles to his feet.*)

SAVAGE. Helen — got to — Helen — Where's she?

MACLUBY. Wrong way.

SAVAGE. Is it? (*He turns to go the other way.*) Can't move with this —

MACLUBY. Solidarity Street.

SAVAGE. Where's that?

MACLUBY. Near the Us Museum.

SAVAGE. Which way's —

MACLUBY. Quick!

SAVAGE (*tugging at the bin*). How can I, with this thing! (*Pause.* SHADE *enters again, with the key to the manacles. He unlocks them.*)

SHADE. Genius can't be encumbered, can it? Genius? (*He goes out again.* SAVAGE *rubs his wrists.*)

MACLUBY. Moon's gone again... (*Pause.*) Never find yer way...

SAVAGE. Free concerts block the avenues...

MACLUBY (*gazing into him*). Unfortunately... (*Pause. Suddenly* SAVAGE *confronts the horror.*)

SAVAGE. All right! (*Pause. He crawls to the mirror* SHADE *has left, and looks in it.*) All right...! (MACLUBY *goes out.*)

Scene Seven

The Street. Sounds of A CONGA. HOGBIN *rushes in.*

HOGBIN. Oi! (THE CONGA *appears, the dancers in sacks.*) Somebody! (*They chant.*)

THE CONGA. Got — to — be — so — glad — now —
Got — to — be — so — glad — now —
Oh — so — glad —
Oh — so — glad —

HOGBIN. Listen, will yer! (*They pass by.*) I must stop doin' that. I shout oi! And no one shifts. Why should they? The Redundant Oi, by Kevin Hogbin. (*He sees* HOMER.) Oi! (*He runs up to him.*) I saw three geezers drag a woman off!

HOMER. The first duty of the poet is to survive. (*Pause.*)

HOGBIN. Is it...? (THE CONGA *returns.*)

THE CONGA. Got — to — be — so — glad — now —
Got — to — be — so — glad — now —
Oh — so — glad —

HOGBIN (*in despair*). Can't think, can yer? **Can't fuckin' think!** (THE CONGA *departs.*)

HOMER. Testament... Not participation...testament!

HOGBIN. An' 'alf of me says 'dance, Kevin! the beat!' An' 'alf says 'put wax in yer ears! Tie down yer feet!'

HOMER. How hard that is! (*He grabs him.*) Listen, my third book.

HOGBIN. **Third** book?

HOMER. I sing you my third book.

HOGBIN. Third book...?

HOMER. Listen, I give it to you! Listen! (*Pause.*) The Heroic Life of the Citizens of Sacked Cities.

HOGBIN. Long title for you.

HOMER (*pause*). The Ruinad. (*Pause.*) I sang it once before. And they left, singly or in groups, like men who had forgotten to post letters, until at the end, I was singing to myself... (*He suddenly sobs.*)

HOGBIN. All right...all right...so what...if it's true — (THE CONGA *reappears.*) **Oh, fuck them...!** (HOMER *begins to sing, but is drowned by* THE CONGA.)

THE CONGA. Got — to — be — so — glad — now —
Got — to — be — so — glad — now —
Oh — so — glad —
Oh — so — glad — (THE CONGA *leaves, except for its last member,* GAY, *who listens.*)

HOMER (*audible now*). You ask me to believe,
You ask me to believe,
In the mercy of the gods,
I say their mercy is only
A refreshment to their malice... (*He fades, falters.*)

HOGBIN. What? (*Pause.* HOMER *is peering blindly, off.*) 'omer? (*Pause.*)
I'm still 'ere. (*Pause.*) As long as one child is 'alf attentive, you 'ave an
audience. (*Pause.*) 'omer. (*Pause.*) **I command the power of your genius!**
The people's right to your imagination...Give us it! (*Pause, then* EPSOM
passes through.)

EPSOM. Old times...Suddenly, what seemed like always and forever, is old
times...

HELEN (*entering, supported by* FLADDER, *and bandaged*). Murder me.
(*She looks round.*) **Murder me.**

HOMER (*who sees nothing*). Murder Helen? Why?

HELEN. **Murder!** (*Pause.*)

HOMER. You don't mean that.

HELEN. I do. I do mean it.

HOMER. Then why ask? There are cliffs. And ponds. Railway tracks, and
dynamos —

HELEN. I want to die —

HOMER. Liar —

HELEN. **Look at me.**

HOMER. **Liar.** (*Pause.*)

HOGBIN (*who has been transfixed by the sight of her wounds*). Giggle...!
Want to giggle...! Try to be grown up but want to giggle...! (*He throws
himself at* HELEN'S *feet, clasping her ankles.*)

GAY. Has anybody got the doctor?

HELEN. It was a doctor did it.

GAY. Oh, good. Oh, good, because... Let's face it, we have seen some awful
things and the presence of trained specialists is comforting...it is! I hate
bad hangmen, for example. Ask the hanged, they will tell you, *merci,
merci,* for a trained professional...! (*She goes to* FLADDER *and puts her
arms round him affectionately.*) She can always grip with her thighs, and
her tongue, which they say is of such great versatility, that could become
as tensile as a cable... (THE BOY *enters, staring.*)

BOY. Woman got no arms... (*They ignore him. He addresses* HOMER.)
Why did you cut her arms off?

GAY. No, it wasn't him...

BOY. Must have been, he —

GAY. No, he only —

BOY. **Yes he did.** (*Pause.*)

HOMER. If I had not made Helen, Helen would not have been disfigured...
(*Pause.*) But Helen had to be made...

GAY. **She did not have to be made!** (*She claps her hand to her mouth.*)
Oh, I —
Oh, I — Now that was — Really, that was so — Outburst in defiance of
all — All right now — (*She is straight, still.*) Still as, and level as, the strand

of sand when tides have all receded...there... (*She smiles, cooly.*) Euphoric Gay. (*She goes out.*)

HOGBIN (*going to* HELEN). Be arms for you. Brush teeth. Rub eyes. And scratch you where you itch. Anticipate every move your invisible limbs would make... (*He encloses her.*)

Interlude

TWO MUSLIMS *enter, with a hamper carried by* A EUROPEAN SERVANT. *They gaze over the country.*

ASAFIR. John, flag please.

YORAKIM. Or someone will take a shot.

ASAFIR. Will pot away.

YORAKIM. And make a shambles of the lunch. (THE SERVANT *erects a white flag.*)

ASAFIR. Thank you, now dish away, I famish, I absolutely famish, oh, look, a skull.

YORAKIM. Trojan.

ASAFIR. Greek.

YORAKIM. The unmistakable long jaw of all —

ASAFIR. The instantly recognizable short forehead of the —

TOGETHER. **We joke like this to keep the horror down.**

YORAKIM. Another flag there, John —

ASAFIR. He's serving lunch —

YORAKIM. Yes —

ASAFIR. He's only got two —

YORAKIM. So he has. Two only. I was thinking, however, is it visible from all the promontories?

ASAFIR. Get a flag yourself. (YORAKIM *stares at* ASAFIR.) All right, I will —

YORAKIM. No, John will. (*Pause.*) I do not think myself better than the servant. That is not the issue. The issue is that in showing myself willing to perform his functions, we —

ASAFIR. I can perfectly well —

YORAKIM. **Erode the basis of service.** (*Pause.*) It would. Erode it.

ASAFIR. Yes, but if, in this instance, a flag of truce would make the crucial difference between life and death —

YORAKIM. **It's false! It's false!**

TOGETHER. **We get like this when drawing lines across the world.**

JOHN (*pointing*). **Terrorists!**

YORAKIM (*spilling his tray*). Fuck...!

JOHN. Hundreds of —

YORAKIM. Oh, fuck...!

ASAFIR (*to* JOHN). The pilchards, please...! (*They sit rigidly on the stools. THE SERVANT serves.*) Ah, pilchards...!

YORAKIM. Oh, Allah —

ASAFIR. Pilchards, I remark —

YORAKIM (*in control*). Yes

ASAFIR. Pilchards, etcetera.

YORAKIM (*seeing* THE TERRORISTS). With knives...!

ASAFIR. The pilchards have knives...?

YORAKIM. **We are in mortal** —

ASAFIR (*to* THE SERVANT). Show them the maps. Shake out the maps. (THE SERVANT *indicates maps. They fall into sheets. He exhibits them.*) Good. Tell them we are of the neutral powers. Tell them we are mappers of the frontier, accredited by the armistice commission, cartographers with no axe to grind. Show them the seals and *laissez passers* of all parties —

YORAKIM. Fuck and fuck —

ASAFIR. We have no weapons but — (THE SERVANT *is demonstrating certificates.*) **Should hands be raised against us we will call down strikes** —

JOHN (*demonstrating*). Crops — **WOOF!**

ASAFIR. And terrible vengeance will be —

JOHN (*miming*). Huts — **WOOF!**

ASAFIR (*to* YORAKIM). Pilchard?

YORAKIM. I think we are going to be killed.

ASAFIR. Not for the first time.

YORAKIM. Not killed for the first time...?

ASAFIR. Not the first time you have —

YORAKIM. I dreamed this.

ASAFIR. I know.

YORAKIM. When I was a child I dreamed this moment —

ASAFIR. We should have asked for guards. In retrospect we obviously should have asked for guards. I thought the flag would speak but clearly it does not. At least not adequately. I do apologize.

YORAKIM (*describing the dream*). I fall to the ground —

ASAFIR. I don't think John is getting anywhere —

YORAKIM. My head is seperated from my body by a single blow —

ASAFIR. Are you, John? Getting anywhere?

YORAKIM. Bounce it goes, and bounce —

ASAFIR. (*standing now*). Thank you, anyway —

YORAKIM (*as* GAY *and* OTHERS *enter, armed*). The unusual perspective of a severed head... (*Pause.*)

GAY. I am going to cut your throats. (*Pause.*)

ASAFIR. Why, for goodness' sake?

GAY (*to* JOHN).And you, collaborator, you will be burned in a dust-bin.

ASAFIR. Make the following points, please —

JOHN (*to* GAY). **I wanted a job, mate.**

ASAFIR. One.

YORAKIM. Get a move on, she —

ASAFIR. One. (*He pauses, wearily.*)

YORAKIM. **Go on, then...!** (*Pause.*)

ASAFIR. No, I don't think there is any point...

GAY. You arrogant and half-dead mannikins.

YORAKIM. You have offended her, and now we shall be most cruelly used.

GAY. In your imperialist silks and turbans spun of slavery...

ASAFIR. I have no political opinions, I am a simple administrator of a frontier line but I will not stoop to plead to a European bitch. There! I have given away my feelings and please do it quickly.

JOHN (*desperately*). **I wanted a job for my Mum whose spine has turned to biscuit — all day she cries in bed** —

GAY. Extenuating gibberish. Many of us suffer but how few of us betray.

JOHN. Many of us don't love our mothers -

GAY. **Oh, burn him quick!** (*They drag him away.*) I think, if we heard all the excuses in the world, no action could occur, and justice would attenuate, an incomprehensible word.

ASAFIR. Not a bad thing, surely?

GAY. **You would say that because you are on top.**

ASAFIR. Admittedly. Such is the yawning gulf between our cultures nothing I say can possibly affect you —

YORAKIM. No —

ASAFIR. Were I possessed of all the wisdom of my race it could not —

YORAKIM (*in despair*). No, no, **wrong argument!**

ASAFIR (*to* YORAKIM). I am not concerned with survival, I am concerned with truth.

GAY. Excellent! Because I shall cut your throats whatever you say. You could be utterly persuasive, logically coherent and morally supreme, and I would still act. **Knife!** (*She holds out a hand to* A FOLLOWER.) Does that fill you with despair?

YORAKIM. Yes...

ASAFIR. No...

YORAKIM. **It fills me with despair.**

ASAFIR. I regard it as the essence of the human condition.

GAY (*triumphantly*). In which case it would be a disappointment if you were spared!

ASAFIR (*conceding*). I am hoist with my own philosophy.

GAY. You are! Now take your funny clothes off, you are dying naked.

ASAFIR. Are we not sufficiently within your power but you —

GAY. **Never sufficiently.** (*Pause.*) Do you think I'll let you die with dignity? Your dignity affronts me. **Strip them if they** — (*They let fall their clothes.*) (*of* YORAKIM.) Take this one away and cut his throat.

ASAFIR. Don't kill my colleague. He is terribly in love with life and —

GAY. **That's why I want to rob him of it.** (*They take him out.*) You really do not understand the nature of revenge. Its satisfactions. Do you?

ASAFIR. No. I just draw maps.

GAY. Your false neutrality.

ASAFIR. I make lines on cartridge paper.

GAY. Your spurious privilege.

ASAFIR. And even as I draw the line I think, this line can't last. Sometimes we draw the line down the middle of a church, and sometimes through a mosque. A dozing drunkard with a reed could mark the frontiers just as well.

GAY. Then why —

ASAFIR. It brings me near the essence of all life. (*Pause. She looks at him for a long time. Then extends the knife to another.*)

GAY. Execute him. Because what he tells me I don't wish to know. (*They lead ASAFIR out.*)

ACT TWO

Prologue

MACLUBY. In the ribbon of green a man is hoeing
Refugees

This one tried wit on thieves
This one tried pity on the police
This one wasted irony on the fanatic

In the ribbon of fertility rich horticulturalists
Dispute the skills of sportsmen

The hours are dying like wasps in the jam
Even blood
Would creep out of an artery
With the stray cat's indolence

And the murdered mistress makes no special noise
She does not beat
She does not hammer with her heels
The hanging gong of the afternoon

The silence of the valley is held breath
The outbreak
Lives in the contingency
The effect of the day's taste in the mouth
Not just the act
But the choice the act included

Sarajevo did not cause the death of fifteen
Million

The theft of Helen did not cause the Siege of Troy

Or Japan's atrocity Hiroshima

No more causes of wars will do

Not just the act
But the choice the act induced

Shh
All peace is stopped breath
Shh
All love's suspension of returning solitude

At night the temple trembles
And the park is tense

Its false orders
Its unearthly symmetry

It knows its chance is brief

We inscribed the fountain as if we believed
This dispensation was eternal
The empire was unshakable
And at the spectacle of culture
Dirty tribesmen would not
                    could not
                    but kneel

Oh, the tomb's false request for exemption
                    This at least
                    This surely must
                    This cannot but command
Your temperance
You yet unborn
You yet to conquer

The cynicism of the generations
Is no less atomizing than the swipe of weapons
Wielded by the hour's enemy

                    That was my only
                    What is that trivial thing to you
                    Your passion for destruction might at
                    Least

The litter of unavailing arguments
A cloud of disbelief in every tongue

Drifts out of cities
Giving earth her rings
More terrible than Saturn

We enter after the siege
We do a little killing

We are not old fashioned
We do not spare the women

We string up the resisters
As we are permitted

We tickle the infant's chin
And watch its sister spitted

And with the draining out of this joyful
Malevolence experience depression such as the
Act of an unequal love induces

We played cards with the survivors
Whose grins were false
I was sorry to detect...

Scene One

SAVAGE *is seated and with authority.*

SAVAGE. My great peace. **Who could like me now?** My restoration. **Who could see me without hatred?** I no longer sit on the edge of the chair. My arse spreads. My arse occupies! **Dr Savage supremely vile, enter all suppliants!** (*He leaps up as a crowd surrounds him.*) Not there! Don't come any nearer! Not there, there! **Silence!** Speak when I indicate you thus — a finger pointed — no shoving — **My wisdom is available to all** — I said no shoving — thus far and no further — **Shut up and still as gargoyles** — (*He points.*) You! (*He feigns attention.*) Mm. (*Pause.*) Mm. (*Pause.*) Mm. (*Pause.*) Enough. The details are — you go on — like an old woman who has the doctor's ear — **Stop.** (*Pause.*) I meditate. (*Pause.*) I pass judgement. Of course the verdict's the source of future quarrel! **Next!** You! Not you! The one with the bulbous nose — **Have you got a bulbous nose?** You have? The physiognomy of Trojan archetypes! The wall-eyed, then. (*Pause.*) Mm. (*Pause.*) Mm. (*Pause.*) Mm. (*As he performs this,* HELEN *enters, watches unseen.*) Mm. (*Pause.*) **Stop!** I meditate. (*Pause.*) I pass judgement. Of course the wrong man suffers! **Next!** You! Not you! The one with jug ears — not you — **Have you got jug ears?** You have? The classic feature of the Trojan race! The hare-lipped, then. (*Pause.*) Mm. (*Pause.*) Mm. (*Pause.*) Mm. (*Pause.*) I tire of — the plethora of ramification — **Precis is the key to justice, stop!** (*He rolls on his knees, laughing, sees* HELEN, *is still. He holds up his hands.*) No bin. (*He stares at her. He claps his hands.* THE SUPPLIANTS *depart.*) The political arrangements of Laughing Troy leave much to be desired but —

(*Pause.*) Always we talk of making a new man but the old man will insist — (*Pause.*) His servile habits — his melancholy aspect — (*Pause.*) And the tendency of poets to crop up like weeds and spread dissent but only for dissension's sake, why? Why? (*Pause.*) Someone is chalking walls with very long words, who? (*Pause.*) And laughter...! You would think sometimes they were pissing milk crates, judging by their rictus jaws. (*Pause.*) There is a medical disorder called Iron Cheek, have you heard? The oiling of the jawbone with whalefat offers some relief but laughter seems to hurt the face as I imagine endless weeping would, it's epidemic and some have died, no one predicted this but — (*He stares at her.*) When you were whole I did not feel for you what — (HOGBIN *appears, skips behind* HELEN.) **Who said he could come in...!** This retinue, this circus of the maimed and callow — it spoils your —

HOGBIN. 'ho says I'm callow? I say you're 'ollow.

SAVAGE. Dignity in suffering!

HOGBIN. You say callow, I say hollow, you say shallow, and I say —

SAVAGE. **Does he have to accompany you at all times of** —

HELEN. Yes. (*Pause.*)

HOGBIN. I say you could 'ave more limbs than an octopus and still not grasp a simple truth, such as—

SAVAGE. **Shut up you** —

HOGBIN. Pity makes your cock big, so pity's only power — **Oi!**

SAVAGE. **I do not see you.** (*Pause.*)

HOGBIN. 'e doesn't see me...

SAVAGE. He does not exist, however present he may be.

HOGBIN. I don't exist...

SAVAGE. Like the butler in the bedroom, or the skivvy at the hearth, to the master you're invisible.

HOGBIN (*screwing himself into a combination of the three monkeys*). I'm invisible... (*Pause.* SAVAGE *grapples with speech.*)

SAVAGE. I have followed you down streets...and where I saw you once...returned...at the same hour...fruitlessly, of course...what is your itinerary...you do presumably go...**I will persist with this**...you have your places but I obviously (*Pause.*) My lungs, my stomach have all gone void and howling with — (*In desperation he extends a hand to her.*) Helen — (*Suddenly* HOGBIN *slaps his face.*)

HOGBIN. There!

SAVAGE (*reeling*). What —

HOGBIN (*darting behind* HELEN). Her arms, not mine! (SAVAGE *makes to grab him.*) **Her arms...!** (*He pretends to scratch* HELEN'S *neck.*)

HELEN. What?

SAVAGE. How can I when —

HELEN. What? (*Pause.*)

SAVAGE. I have to be your lover. I who invented your condition **Must.** (*Pause.*)

HELEN. To be my lover? And what is that? (*Pause.*)

SAVAGE. What is it...?

HELEN. **What is it, yes!**

HOGBIN (*to* SAVAGE). Are you deaf or something? You talk about the beginning and she wants to know the end. (SAVAGE *reaches out. Again* HOGBIN *beats his hand away.* SAVAGE *reels.*) Thinks to finger me. Thinks to touch specific parts will weaken all resistance. He's read a book on the erogenous zones which says the touch kills argument.

SAVAGE. Help me.

HOGBIN. **Help you? Help you?**

SAVAGE. I twist. I writhe. I'm poisoned. Mind of slab of concrete and the minutes hang off me like crankshafts, I could snap the hands off clocks they move so sullenly, **The length of a night,** do you know **the impossible duration of a single night,** I lick the clouds for dawn, and cats, I know their tracks and habits, the wriggle of the tomcat's arse and all the lashing of dawn choruses, **It hurts to look at you,** I would chuck imagination in the ditch and bury it for one moment of your sad mouth against my sad mouth — (*He sees* HOGBIN'S *expression.*) **What's he to you, the grinning bastard?** (*He bites his lip. Pause.*)

HELEN. Nothing new. (*Pause.*)

SAVAGE. No...

HELEN. In your message. (*Pause.*)

SAVAGE. Well, no...

HELEN. Is there?

SAVAGE. I suppose there wouldn't be —

HELEN. Nothing new in that. (*Pause.*) Why maim me? (*Pause.*) **I was already a spectacle of pain, why else did they want me?** (SAVAGE *stares at her.*) Beauty did you say? No, it's pain they loved... (HOGBIN'S *hands reach up to* SAVAGE'S *face, and hold him.*) My kiss is stiff as brick, and my womb full of straw...but he won't mind... (*He draws* SAVAGE *to* HELEN'S *breast.*) Arid Helen...But he won't mind... (SAVAGE *shudders.*) Listen, his male murmur, his male thirst... (CREUSA *enters, looks.*)

CREUSA. Who needs arms to fasten in their buttocks? (*Pause.*)

HOGBIN. I can't see you today...

CREUSA. **I'll thrust my arms in a reaping machine, will that make me popular?** (*Pause.*)

HOGBIN. I can't see you today...

CREUSA. Well, no, you've got work to do. **Should I stuff my arse in a shredder?**

SAVAGE (*catching a sound*). Shh! (*Pause.*)

CREUSA. Mums' Troy.

SAVAGE. Shh!

CREUSA. I plant it like a seed. Mums' Troy. It sprouts. It blooms. It sends out runners.

SAVAGE (*getting to his feet*). Listen! (*Pause. He cups his ear.*) No laughter...

HOGBIN (*straining his ear*). No drums.

SAVAGE. Or rattles. **The tambourine has ceased, hey!**

SHADE (*running in*). **Silence...! Where's it coming from?**

HOGBIN (*pointing arbitrarily*). There... (EPSOM *and* GUMMERY *hurry in.*)

SHADE (*indicating*). There! (EPSOM *rushes in the direction*.)

HOGBIN. No, there! (GUMMERY *looks in bewilderment, and* EPSOM *returns, blankly*.)

EPSOM. Hold it...

SHADE. Noises are starting in my head. The whispering of shared and subtle sacraments. Start a carnival! (*No one moves. Pause*.) I hear the little stirring of the private act. Make the bands play! (*Still no one moves. Realisation dawns on* SHADE. *He walks slowly across the stage, stops*.) The word today is — (*Suddenly, as if impulsively,* GUMMERY *seizes* SHADE *in his arms, pinioning him and lifting him off the ground*.)

GUMMERY. No word!

SHADE. Oh, Brian, you — Oh, Brian, you magnificent specimen, I twitch in your embrace as the helpless hamster in the infant's fingers. **But to what effect!** (*Pause*.) All right, I'll have a tantrum. (*He kicks his legs like a baby*.) Tantrum, all right? Now, can we get back to politics, we have a state to govern. (*Pause*.)

GUMMERY. What shall I do? (*He turns to anyone who will listen*.) What shall I do? (*Pause*.)

SHADE. Come on, Brian, they will be missing you in the gymnasium. Put me down, will you. (*Pause*.)

GUMMERY. I can't put you down.

SHADE. You can't? Why not?

GUMMERY. Because I picked you up.

SHADE. What? Logic! Logic! Can't put me down because you — logic! Logic!

GUMMERY. I picked you up to stop you, and if I put you down you'll start again. So I can't put you down. (*Pause*.)

SHADE. Well, Brian, you have a problem. It comes of making gestures that you can't complete.

EPSOM. Put him down if he promises to —

SHADE. **No deals.**

EPSOM. Barry, you ain't in much of a position to —

SHADE. **I am in the best position. I have the brain.** (*Pause*.) Really, who would credit this? People don't know how they're governed.

GUMMERY (*to* EPSOM). I don't know what to do...

SHADE. You don't, do you? You really don't.

GUMMERY. Les? (EPSOM *shrugs*.)

SHADE. No luck with Les.

GUMMERY. **Shuddup will yer!** (*Pause*.)

SHADE. I won't ask if your arms are aching because you are in such wonderful condition no doubt you could keep this up for weeks, I only ask you, in all humbleness, do you know what you're doing? (*Pause*.)

GUMMERY. No.

SHADE. Excellent. Point of departure. Now, put me on the ground and we —

CREUSA. No —

SHADE. What?

CREUSA. No —

SHADE. Come again —

CREUSA. Don't —

SHADE. Brian, this is a Trojan bitch —

CREUSA. Put him down and they'll hate you in every bar between the dockyards and the allotments —

SHADE. Brian —

CREUSA. Women will knit your shape in wool and men throw darts at it —

SHADE. Listen, we fought ten years for one whore, don't let another —

CREUSA. **Keep him up, I said.**

SHADE. **Come on, Doctor, it's your government!** (*Pause.*) Oh doctor... I think you wear silence like a tart wears frocks, half off the shoulder...to make more appetizing the hagflesh underneath...**Anything underneath?** (*Pause.*)

SAVAGE. I must betray you, do you mind? (*Pause.*) I am a traitor by instinct, because to doubt is treason, and I doubt commitment even as I utter it, whether to women or the state. Have you not noticed, I write constitutions as boys make planes from glue and balsa? (*Pause.*) And now you ache to punish me. I do understand that, the thirst for punishment, I do know disloyalty burns the stomach to a cinder. (*Pause.*) Don't put him down, he'll only ram sharp things in our eyes...

Scene Two

FLADDER, *seated, weaves a massive basket.*

HELEN. When you lost your tongue, did you stop thinking? (*He looks at her.*) The contrary, of course. (*Pause.*) And so with me. (*Pause.*) **Armless I still reach out, why?** (*Pause. He works.*) I tell you this because you are my husband. Come what may, this fuck or that, this famine or this riot, you are my husband. (*Pause.*) Funny word. I think it mean, like old domestic dog, or cat, **had teeth once. Was wild in certain states.** (*He stops.*) Oh, don't weep. **Don't weep I honour you.** (*Pause.*) All right, not honour, I don't honour you. I retail my life. (*Pause.*) **Who else should I tell?** I am carrying the doctor's child. (*Pause.*) I think. (*Pause.*) Do do the raffia. Weave on. (*Pause. She spontaneously goes to him, nuzzles his head.*) Oh, you must have developed so much in your silence, I think if your late wisdom was inscribed I'd say, **Brilliant but utterly incomprehensible!** So remote you are, so distant from our — (CREUSA *appears.* HELEN *turns to face her.*) Don't pester me, I can still kick.

CREUSA. Answer —

HELEN. You bother like a barmy wasp — you cling —

CREUSA. Answer —

HELEN. **What is it, jam on my lip?**

CREUSA. **Why aren't you ashamed of your life? I insist you're ashamed of your life.** (*Pause.*) I think my cunt drips acid and if he were to enter me I'd scald the seven skins off him, **Whose child is it,** I make a fool of myself, obviously, an utter fool, they say the ex-queen's cracked, half her head's turned biscuit, and then I think, a fool, so what, a fool to who? I won't stuff hatred down, a little wire sawing away inside my gut and grin all rights, I won't! (*Pause.*)

HELEN. He stands behind me.

CREUSA. Yes.

HELEN. And close.

CREUSA. Go on.

HELEN. His belly — you want to know this, do you —

CREUSA. Yes —

HELEN. To my arse and so — (*Pause.*)

CREUSA. Go on — please — (*Pause.*)

HELEN. No more.

CREUSA. **More. Yes!**

HELEN. You want the pain. You want it...how you want... (*Pause.*)

CREUSA. The hate grows on my gums at night. Thick paste of loathing. I spit it in the sink. (HOGBIN *enters gaily.*)

HOGBIN (*holding them out*). Washed our hands! (*(He sees* CREUSA, *stops. She goes out.*)

HELEN. Twelve Troys! (*He goes to feed her from a bowl.*) Twelve Troys and then —

HOGBIN. Egg mayonnaise!

HELEN. Twelve Troys and then what?

HOGBIN. Twelve?

HELEN. Twelve, yes. And me to suffer under every one! (*Pause. He stares at her.*)

HOGBIN (*thrusting it to her lips*). Brown bread —

HELEN. **No bread!**

HOGBIN. Egg, then —

HELEN. **No egg!**

HOGBIN. Must eat —

HELEN. Why eat? To live? For what? For love? Whose love?

HOGBIN. Yer going on —

HELEN. Your love? **I have no arms! I watch, I listen, Helen has nine Troys to suffer, all right, I eat, all right, the bread, the egg, I persevere, shh!** (*He feeds her.*)

GAY (*entering*). **Mums' Troy.** The first lesson. (*Pause.*) I am not a mum. But I did write the lesson. (*Pause.*) In the first place was the **Aristocracy,** and they were so idle they gave away their infants to others to suckle, so the infants grew up most confused regarding love, not distinguishing their mothers from their nurses or their arses from their lips, and consequently **plundered the world with icy hardness.** And after them came the **Democrats,** who believed life was too short for privilege, so they sent their infants into **schools** to learn the way of the world, and they emerged from schools like tigers, intent on butchering the **weak**. And finally there came the **Loving Mothers,** who kept their infants close, breathing the breath of the child and sleeping its sleep, so each single child grew up full of certainty the world loved her, which it did, to some extent. But so did all the others, **Love's a drug, you see,** and they tore each other to ribbons in their jealousy! (*Pause.*) Unofficial version. (*A thunderous noise.*)

48 *Howard Barker*

Scene Three

SHADE, *imprisioned in the woven basket, is raised by pulleys drawn by* EPSOM *and* GUMMERY. SAVAGE *watches.*

SHADE. Oh, dear, I shall get wet...! The piss of Zeus will shrink me like a garment, sodden one minute and bleached the next **I like it here incidentally** I'll shrivel until this little floor is vast as plains which take me days to scuttle over **I always wanted this, didn't you know?** My longing to be stopped — (*He touches the sides.*) Edge! Edge! **Oh, lovely limit to my dream!** Goodbye, Brian, and goodbye, Les, I shrink, you great empire builders, *au revoir,* I have my provinces as well, **What's Rome to a galaxy? What's Russia in the sun? Speck, Brian, Speck!** (*He is still.* GUMMERY *and* EPSOM *leave.* SAVAGE *watches the basket.*)
SAVAGE. Because I was an intellectual I chose to follow thought, thought to the finish, that is the duty of one, isn't it? The finger of thought beckoned me past the frontier post where others who had been my equals stood or waved me through, **Yes, you stay behind and court your admirers**, oh, the teachers with their followings, the gifted with their cliques, they carve their names in wet cement to the sound of the acolyte's giggles, **Dance on the skin of knowledge** but don't fall through, you'll drop forever. (*Pause.*) Helen! (*Pause.*) It howls here and no cunning girls of seventeen think I am fascinating, no youths can be seduced in my dim study or learn the trivial habits of depravity over set texts, **Knickers and Kafka, Saliva and The Greeks! Helen!** (*She enters, with* HOGBIN, *looks at him.*)
HELEN. Oh, my ugly lover...
SAVAGE. Yes...
HELEN. Oh, my shapeless adorer, would you hack my legs off also? Legless, would you desire me more?
SAVAGE. I don't...
HELEN. You do know, yes, you do...
SAVAGE. I don't...
HELEN. **What part, then...!** (*He hides his face.*) What joint or knuckle, what pared-down, shredded, particle would serve to be the point at which your love would say stop, **Essential Helen?** Slithering over rocks, some sliver of cheek or gum, there! Saw her! Flap of appendix in the rock pool! (*He goes to reach for her.*) Don't come near me. The greater the space between us, the more I suffer. It conducts my heat. She tells me I must be ashamed. I'm unashamed. And so are you. Twice the dead of Troy and I would not apologize. I have your child or maybe not, all this and unashamed. (*He goes to reach for her.*) Don't come nearer...! You will kill my ecstasy! (*He stops.*) They hate me in Mums' Troy, they hate me worse than ever Shade or Fladder did, can it be true that every life is precious, can it? Mums' Troy is babies, all the kerbs are padded and the rivers hung with nets, breasts out in the market and the endless music of their gurgles, the **preposterous claim of life —**

SAVAGE. Kiss me —

HELEN. Your squirt, my fluid, look out, **Claims from the muddy water!** They all want their ninety years and I brought whole regiments to earth like flies on wallpaper...

SAVAGE. Kiss me —

HELEN. **The Snail's insistence on its rights!** (*She halts him.*) If I saw a baby drift by on a raft of rushes I would not lift a finger for it, though the river bubbled it to sharks or iceflows, pity, the great unending ribbon of pity, it has no end except exhaustion, I have a child in me and yet I hacked the features off dying boys, and I have watched priests visit the starving whilst eating sandwiches, but listen, the doctor must be fed! The doctor must eat even if the patient starves, that's logical! All this logic! All this pity! Kiss me, now. Kiss me...! (*He kisses her.*) Your mouth would draw me in and make me vanish, a sweet in your jaw, sucked to oblivion... (*They kiss.*)

HOGBIN (*withdrawing from their embrace*). Nine Troys to go...!

GAY (*off*). Psst!

HOGBIN. Wha'?

GAY. Psst!

HOGBIN. Where! (*He stares in the dark.*) Can't see yer, here —

GAY (*emerging*). Got to have a baby.

HOGBIN. Got to 'ave a —

GAY. You'll do.

HOGBIN. Me? What 'ave you —

GAY (*jerking her skirt up*). Like this —

HOGBIN. Hold on —

GAY. **What for.** (*She glares at him.*) New Troy's for babies. So. (*Pause.*)

HOGBIN. Look I —

GAY. **What!** (*Pause.*)

HOGBIN. No will. And no desire. Sorry.

GAY. Look, pregnant women get three ration books. That's will. I got my legs open. That's desire. Now do it.

HOGBIN. I can't just —

GAY. **You are interfering with my happiness.** (*Pause.*) The happiness I'm entitled to, you are frustrating it.

HOGBIN. Ask someone else.

GAY. I have done. I just asked Homer. Homer can't.

HOGBIN. He can't!

GAY. Apparently he can't. He wept. Absurd. And he's been pestering me for years. (*Pause. He looks away.*) Really, if you were a dog, you would. Have you seen dogs? (*He shakes his head.*) If you don't, I'm down the harbour. (*Pause. She turns swiftly.*)

HOGBIN. Don't do that.

GAY. Why not? Lots of dogs down there, in sailors' outfits, woof! (*She laughs. Then she puts her arms round his neck. Sound of infantile wailing.*)

Scene Four

GUMMERY, EPSOM *enter with babies under each arm, which they place on the ground.*MACLUBY *enters, passing* HOGBIN, OTHERS, *also carrying babies. The stage rapidly fills with babies, as the carriers come and go.*

MACLUBY. The land restocked. (*They gurgle.* CREUSA *brings two further armfuls.*) The terrible regime of innocence. (*And others.*) Its jurisprudence.

CREUSA. **Why fucking not.**

MACLUBY (*shrugs*). No reason.

CREUSA. No reason. And who wants it? Reason brought us to extinction's edge. **No reason in Mums' Troy.** (*Babies are filling the stage.*) We found a scientist and made him sweep the street. He swept the street but chalked formulae on kerbs. So we gave him lavatories to swab. He swabbed the lavatories but made secret drawings on the underside of seats. So we executed him. It is a sickness, curiosity.

EPSOM (*putting down* A BABY). 'oo's a little baby, then, 'oo's a little —

CREUSA. You are mocking that child.

EPSOM. Am I? Sorry.

CREUSA. The child is your superior.

EPSOM. Yup.

CREUSA. A moral genius compared to you.

EPSOM. Yup.

CREUSA (*to* GAY). Gay, please.

GAY. The Second Lesson of Mums' Troy.

CREUSA. Louder. They will be silent if you interest them. They will be attentive if you win their respect.

GAY. Yes... (*She clears her throat.*) **The Second Lesson of Mums' Troy.**

CREUSA. A baby is not a baby.

GAY. No.

CREUSA. It is an adult in a state of moral excitement.

GAY. Yes.

CREUSA. Go on.

GAY. Innocence is not without authority! Nor does purity go unarmed! The meaningless violence of Old Troys is replaced by the liberating force of pre-articulacy — (*To* CREUSA.) They aren't listening —

CREUSA. Oh, yes, they are —

GAY. Are they?

CREUSA. Go on —

GAY (*louder*). Spared language but also spared — (*She turns to* CREUSA *in despair.*) I can't seem to make them —

CREUSA. You are imposing oppressive notions of silence and discipline on them. They are engrossed —

GAY (*puzzled*). They're —

CREUSA. **Engrossed.** (*She stamps her foot on the ground.*) **Shhh.** (*Silence. Pause.*) Where's Helen? (EPSOM *looks at* GUMMERY.) Fetch Helen, please. (*They go out. Gurgles of contentment fill the stage.* CREUSA *walks up and down between* THE BABIES. HELEN *appears, with* SAVAGE. *Pause.*) Helen, where's your baby? (*Pause.*) Ask you again. (*Pause.*)Where's your baby? (*Pause.* THE BABIES *begin to fret.*) Oh, God, they sense catastrophe... (*She stamps her foot. Silence.*) Helen, is your baby still alive? (*Pause.* THE BABIES *start to cry.*) Oh, they cry with horrible anticipation...!

SAVAGE. She —

CREUSA. **Shut up, you.** Helen, have you...terrible to speak this but...have you...awful but we must endure...

SAVAGE. She is the —

CREUSA. **Shut up, you!** (*Pause.*) Betrayed the sacred trust of motherhood...? (*Pause.*) Have you, my dear? (*She stamps her foot.* THE BABIES *are still.*)

HELEN. It died.

CREUSA. Of what?

HELEN. Insignificance. (THE BABIES *screech.*)

GUMMERY. **Mur — der!**

HELEN. You should know.

CREUSA. You stifled innocence. You hung a cloth over its face.

HELEN. Innocence? No, it was guilty. They all are.

CREUSA. Of what?

HELEN. Aborting love.

CREUSA (*to a rage of* BABIES). They accuse! They prosecute!

GAY (*ignoring* THE COURT, *to* HOGBIN). Love you.

HOGBIN. Wha'?

GAY. Love you!

HELEN. The more you sin yourselves, the more you must insist on innocence, you impose it on your infants.

CREUSA. **To kill you own child...**

HELEN. It would have been a killer, too, of the love I suffer for its father. I never let a child come in the way of love. You know the appetite of babies. And this one was voracious. (THE BABIES *strike new notes.*) Half my sons slew men they never knew, and half my daughters slept with murderers...!

CREUSA. You stuffed a pillow on its face!

HELEN. I was more charitable than that.

CREUSA. How, then?

HELEN. I did it with my breast. (THE BABIES *are stunned with horror.*) A breast is milk, but also, pillow...

EPSOM. Brian, I think I will be sick...

GUMMERY. A mother kills her — I can't say it — with 'er — I can't say it —

GAY (*to* HOGBIN). We'll grow old together! I'll be an old apple, and you'll be an old pear...!

EPSOM. We should 'ave murdered 'er! (*He comforts a nearby* BABY.) Oochie, coochie, coochie... When she stood in the ruins of Old Troy — oochie, coochie! Murdered her!

CREUSA (*walking among* THE BABIES). Some want revenge...but others...call for clemency...

HELEN. The hate...

CREUSA. Not hate...

HELEN. Hate, wordlessly. What they would not give for a word! And we, who have words, **scream...**

CREUSA. Call for clemency, from there... (*She indicates* A BABY.) He argues...

EPSOM. It's a she.

CREUSA. She persuades. She is most effective. And they (*she indicates all* THE OTHERS.) agree! Your plea —

HELEN. I made no plea —

CREUSA. Your plea finds sympathy! I am so happy for you! (*Pause.*) But at the same time — our disapproval must be registered. The act may be forgiven, but it must be marked... (*Pause. She walks among* THE BABIES.) How quiet they are, not vindictive, but melancholy, philosophical...

HELEN. Oh, listen...the prelude to my pain...

SAVAGE. Helen!

HELEN. The gulf of imagination yawns...

SAVAGE. Helen! (*Pause.* CREUSA *moves silently among* THE BABIES. *Stops. Pause.*)

CREUSA. They ask...in all humility...for him who suffers most...to choose...(*She looks at* SAVAGE. HELEN *lets out a terrible laugh. Pause.*)

HOGBIN. Hold it...

CREUSA. Shut up...

HOGBIN. Not 'im, not 'im, 'e's —

HELEN (*to* HOGBIN). **You stifle him. His mind. Its dream. You trample him.** (*Pause.*)

SAVAGE. They say... (*Pause.*) If I interpret them... (*Pause.*) You have failed to be a mother, and therefore should not look like one... (THE BABIES *screech.*) **I said it! I said it!**

CREUSA (*to* EPSOM, GUMMERY). Out — quick — and do it!

HELEN. Oh, I'll be good! Oh, this time, promise! I'll be good!

HOGBIN (*to* SAVAGE). **Maniac!**

SAVAGE. Don't you want to know! Oh, don't you **want!**

HOGBIN. Helen! (EPSOM *and* GUMMERY *lead* HELEN *away.*)

SAVAGE. You want to save her. But she can't be saved. **I know what Helen is.** (HOGBIN *hurries after.*) She could have reared the child in a garden. She could have stayed in Greece. **Always the possibility of silent life but..** (*He walks through* THE BABIES.) And he throws his pity at her, like confetti in a hurricane...

CREUSA. You know too much.

SAVAGE. Yes.

CREUSA. **Do you know you can know too much.**

SAVAGE. Yes. I know even that. (*Pause.* THE BABIES *begin complaining.*)

CREUSA (*to* THE ADULTS). Clear them out. (THE ADULTS *collect up the bundles and carry them away.* SAVAGE *sees* MACLUBY.)

SAVAGE. How many selves have we got, MacLuby? (MACLUBY *looks at him.*) Old self, grab it, can we? Old self off the shelf? (*He stops.*) Show us an old self, MacLuby!

MACLUBY. Trembling...

SAVAGE. Yes...

MACLUBY. Shuddering...

SAVAGE. Yes, but not with horror! How you would love that!

MACLUBY. Me? No.

SAVAGE. How philistine and trite! My grappling with conscience, my submission and supine apology, suicide from a borrowed rope, no. (MACLUBY *shrugs, sets off.*) Show us an old self. (*He stops.*)

MACLUBY. Wants to reach into the wardrobe —

SAVAGE. Yes —

MACLUBY. Take an old self off the hanger —

SAVAGE. Yes —

MACLUBY. Blow the dust off and —

SAVAGE. Why not? How else can I see if I've travelled? (*Pause.* SAVAGE'S SON *enters. They stare at one another.*)

BOY (*tossing a bar of soap*). Ashes of roses... (*Pause.*)

SAVAGE. What...?

BOY. Ashes of roses... (*Pause.*)

SAVAGE. Good... (CREUSA *enters, gesticulating wildly to* EPSOM *and* GUMMERY.)

CREUSA. He said —

EPSOM. We 'eard what he said —

CREUSA. **He said — She was not a Mother —**

GUMMERY. We —

CREUSA. **Listen — exact words — Therefore she should not look like one —**

EPSOM. She doesn't —

CREUSA. **What!**

EPSOM. She doesn't look like one. (*Pause of exasperated disbelief. To* GUMMERY.) Does she? (GUMMERY *shakes his head.*)

CREUSA. What's a mother got?

EPSOM. What's a —

CREUSA. **Yes, what?** (*They stare at one another in bewilderment.* CREUSA *tears open her garment.*) **It's breasts she's got!** (*Pause.*)

EPSOM (*at the point*). We'll go back and — (CREUSA *catches sight of* THE BOY, *standing. She stares at him. Pause.*) Shall we? (*She goes to him, smells his hair, his skin. Pause. She sits on the ground.*) Go back and — (*She does not reply. A wind grows from a whisper.*)

Scene Five

HOGBIN *enters with a dish on a pole, which he extends to the cage. He waits. He grows impatient.*

HOGBIN. Dinn — er! (*The wind. Pause.*) Dinn — er! (*Pause. He puts down the pole, flashes his torch at the cage. It is empty. He turns the torch off, then on again. He falls heavily to the floor.*) **Ed — u — cat — tion!** (*He seizes the pole. Wields it.*) Against irrationality the pole of knowledge! **Off!** (*He prods at the air. Pause. He approaches the cage.*) Are you in there? (*Pause.*) Are you, though...? (*Pause.*) Come again...? (*Pause. HOGBIN emits a cry of horror. A tiny laugh from the cage. He sinks to the floor. Daylight.* HELEN *enters, armless, legless, pushed by* HOMER *in a chair.*)

HELEN. I've missed you! I really have! I went to brush my hair, and where were my arms? I went to get out of bed, and where were my legs? Fortunately my creator appeared and lent me limbs, but he can't do a woman justice as you can, look, he's got my blouse on back to front. I didn't criticise. He is at least a hundred, aren't you. One hundred at least. Gay says you love each other, but how can you, there is nothing to love, or do you love that? Do you love her vacancy and plan to write your signature across her void? My stumps hurt when the wind is in the East, which is the prevailing angle **The more they injure me the more they hate,** can you explain that? You're educated. (*He looks at her.*) They want to pity me, it is their only hope, but I am not pitiful, am I? I cannot think why they neglect my face, it is the obvious starting point, but perhaps they need to see me weep. I do weep. Or shout an accusation. They long to be accused. **I won't satisfy them.** (*Pause.*) My clothes are so exquisite, I found a woman who understands the trunk, as form, its own aesthetic, and her hemming is magnificent. I think in future we shall all be mutants, we shall be born so, and all limbs will be knobs, and some will have more, and some will have less, and there will be such a wonderful variety! It will happen in the womb, how I don't know, some fine powder will fall from the sky, or something in the water, and we will be such a fascinating menagerie! I set this fashion, as I did in Attica, I was slavishly copied there, but now I am rather too progressive. Do you know what Doctor Savage says, he says I am two mouths, that's all. **Two mouths!** And I ran every morning in Old Troy. While Paris kipped his coital kip I was up and tearing through the market, the porters' bawdy in the slipstream of my arse! They pelted me with fruit and once I let them cluster me, on sacks. But only once. Royalty is loved for its transgressions but not habitually. (*Pause.*) Are you deserting me? (*Pause.*)

HOGBIN. I am losing my mind...

HELEN. Which mind? The one you brought to Troy with you?

HOGBIN. **Which mind?**

HELEN. Yes. Which? Do you think you lose your mind? You find others. Do you think you lose your sight? You see by other channels. And the legless also manoeuvre! I once saw a fingerless woman with twelve inch thumbs. **Of course I say this to console myself.** (*Pause.*) You want your mind, but why? To document your pain? To put order in it? To fix its mayhem, why? **Welcome Pain I always was expecting you.** Even in copulation, even in the madness of torrential fuck I knew my agony awaited me. Is Gay delivered of monster yet?

HOGBIN. It's not a monster.

HELEN. How do you know?

HOGBIN. Because we're healthy.

HELEN. Healthy? What's health to do with it? Of course it is a monster but it merely lacks the strength **Shh! I was punished for saying this last month, Shh!** (*She looks at* HOMER.) This man is a monster, aren't you?

HOMER. Yes.

HELEN. I believe he would torture the world to death, for disappointment.

HOMER. Yes.

HELEN. Poets' Troy will be the worst yet. **Poets' Troy, duck you innocents!** (*Pause. To* HOGBIN.) Hold me, and tell me what I feel like. I cannot hold myself.

HOGBIN. I can't.

HELEN. Why ever not?

HOGBIN. I'll only — I'll get all — start to —

HELEN. Go on, then —

HOGBIN. No.

HELEN. **Hold me...!** (*He goes to her, puts his arms round her. Pause.*)

HOGBIN. I want —

HELEN. What? What do you want?

HOGBIN. A clean, white shirt... (*Pause.*) A tie... (*Pause.*) And trousers, with a perfect crease... (*Pause.*)

HOMER. When Troy fell I followed Odysseus. I followed him because I could not bring myself to look into the ruins. We all knew, there was a history in the ruins. But I thought, there will be no public for a song about the ruins...

HOGBIN. **It's your job, you bastard.** (*Pause.* CREUSA *enters.*)

CREUSA. Your wife's in labour. (HOGBIN *detaches himself from* HELEN, *starts to go.*) The Mums are in attendance. But you may wait. You wait, and pace. Up and down, you pace. Your painless hours. Pitiable thing. (*He goes out. To* HELEN *with joy.*) Another baby! (*Pause.*) My son appeared.

HELEN. Did he?

CREUSA. As if to cleanse me. My lost son. As if to make the juice of kindness flow from my dry and withered ducts. Tears from the baked kernels of my eyes. As if, flinging our arms about each other we would cry, 'Forgive...!'

HELEN. And...?

CREUSA. And I would be washed in pity and walk with a serenity I never found in all my kicked-up life...

HELEN. But...?

CREUSA. It isn't like that. (*Pause. Then* HELEN *laughs.*) Yes, do laugh. You know, don't you, it isn't like that? The redemption? The reunion? All lies? (HELEN *laughs.*) She knows, she knows better than you! (*She looks at* HOMER.) **Redemption fuck.** (*Pause.*) No, we change, we do change. There's the misery. Except for you. (*Pause.*) He told them, tear your breasts off. But they made a torso out of you instead. Men don't grasp metaphors, do they? Not swift to connect. Under the circumstances the babies recommend you may keep the rest —

HELEN. I thank the babies —

CREUSA. Do you?

HELEN. Profusely. (*Pause.*)

CREUSA. I think even as you say a thing, you know it to be false. You know it, and yet you say it. I think you are the enemy of all Troys no matter whose. I think you believe nothing and therefore ought to suffer everything imagination might conceive. **I am a better person than you.**

HELEN. Yes.

CREUSA. However cruel.

HELEN. Yes.

CREUSA. For all the rotting of my kindness and the crumbling of my soul —

HELEN. Yes —

CREUSA. **I am. I am.** (*Pause. She runs to* HELEN, *holds her.*) Oh, you sliced thing, you make me **shudder.** (*To* HOMER.) Dosen't she? Make you **shudder?** (*She caresses* HELEN.) Say you deserved it, say you earned it, say it, say...

HELEN. Yes...

CREUSA. I cannot resist you. I, the better person, cannot resist you, why? When you are so incorrigible, why? This terrible but honest place. This island of confessions. I long for you, and my son is earth, is pebble. (*To* HOMER.) Can you explain that? (*He shakes his head.*) **He doesn't want to know any more..** (*She lovingly undoes* HELEN'S *buttons.*) And he puts her blouse on back to front...

Scene Six

SAVAGE *is sitting under the cage.*

SAVAGE. So Alexander the Great came to the barrel where Diogenes was living **Fuck knows why he lived in a barrel the poseur** and said I am the most powerful man in the world, come to listen to you, the wisest man in the world, speak. And the yob waited. The yob waited for the poseur. And Diogenes said, timing this equisitely, and **with all the calculation of a man who knew no autocrat would stoop to tear his bowels out,** the poseur said, **believing himself secure in his reputation as five Persian armies behind their stakes,** said, **You have to admire the predictability, you really do,** you are standing in my sunlight. (*Pause.*) **Do you call that wit! Do you call that insolence?** (*Pause. A tiny laugh from the cage.*) The intellectual Bajcsy-Zsilinsky had been a racist murderer, an anti-semite, a killer of trade unionists, a scrawler of slogans, a publisher of slanders, an editor of intimidating magazines, anti-pity, anti-intellect, but when the Nazis came he met them with a gun. **He had truly travelled.** And they shot shot him in a cellar. **Bang**. The futility of acquiescence versus the futility of resistance. **Bang.** Why are you dressed like an accountant? (HOGBIN *has* *entered, and waits.*) Are there accountants in Mums' Troy? How can there be when there's no money? But no, that's logical, that's symmetry, the increase in the level of poverty will be matched by the rise in students of accountancy, and as for poverty we recommend more barrels! (*Pause.*) No, you're worried, I can see you are. I go on, and you're worried. I humour myself and you fret. **That's how we are, John!** I pretend. I act sympathy. (*He pretends to listen.*) The ear — extended. (*Pause.*)

HOGBIN. It ain't normal. (*Pause.*)

SAVAGE. Ah.

HOGBIN. **It ain't normal.**

SAVAGE. Pity...perhaps...

HOGBIN. They say it's me.

SAVAGE. Who does?

HOGBIN. The Babies.

SAVAGE. Say it's you...?

HOGBIN. I said why don't yer let me see it, they said just stand there, I said you're hiding something they said wait, I said it's my kid too, you — and I released a torrent of abuse —

SAVAGE. Well, naturally —

HOGBIN. I was that tense —

SAVAGE. Inevitably —

HOGBIN. And I saw it, and it was — (*Pause.*) They say I am a genetic criminal. (*Pause.*) What's that? (GAY *enters, sits. Long pause.*)

GAY. I do not love it. (*Pause.*) How I wanted to... (*Pause.*) And how absurd to want.

HOGBIN. **A genetic criminal, what's that!** Gay, you testify —

GAY. The testicles can testify.

HOGBIN. Gay —

GAY. **Shh, I am the teacher!** (*Pause.*) Because I know, and always knew, to be born was absurd. So absurd that to be angry was equally absurd. And just as being angry was absurd, so caring was absurd. Quite as absurd. Which left me only — ecstasy. Not my mother's ecstasy, not the fucking-out of consciousness — but the different ecstasy of perpetuating absurdity because what else can you do when you are the victim of a joke but participate in the joke and so outjoke the joker? **Laugh louder, always louder still.** So birth was ecstasy. Through the red blankets of pain I applauded all the blind and inexorable circumstances that brought life into this sticky planet. **More life! And more life yet!** (*Pause.*)

HOGBIN. We'll find a shack. I'll put some flowers round the —

GAY. If only it were malice! The surge of mud that — the earthquakes that — the flood which suffocates the infant and the murderer. If only it were malice...but it isn't...how intolerable...How impossible to assimilate... (*Pause.*) So of course you're guilty. You have to be. And I have to hate. (*She extends a hand to him.*) What's your innocence got to do with it? (*He takes her hand.*) Hide, then. (*She shouts.*) **The Criminal is touching me!** Hide...!

HOGBIN. Gay —

GAY. **Pol — ice!**

HOGBIN. **Hide where?**

SAVAGE. And so, to hide him from his enemies, Athene wrapped him in a
mist...

HOGBIN. Give us a mist, then!

GAY. **Pol — ice!**

HOGBIN (*running one way, then back again*). Mist...! Mist...? No mist!

SAVAGE. Opinion.

HOGBIN. Wha'?

GAY (*hurrying out*). **The Criminal Enemy of Mums' Troy!** (*She points to*
HOGBIN.)

SAVAGE. **Opinion** — (*men rush in with sticks*) **is — the — mist.** (HOGBIN
turns to face them. A fraction of calculation elapses.)

HOGBIN. Helen did it. (*They stop.*)

I mean.

I mean, the misery that woman's.

I mean, her life continues in the same old.

I mean, the very sight of her.

I ask you. (*Pause.*) I am the Accountant and therefore the disposer of all
life and death, all marriage, surgery and literacy off my calculation, yes,
even the colour of the woman's pants and the baby's rash (*Pause.*) She is
guilty, you know that as well as me —

EPSOM. I 'ave chopped 'er twice, son —

HOGBIN. And is that sufficient? Two?

GUMMERY. Stood in her blood —

HOGBIN. I ask you. I don't seek to persuade, I merely ask —

GUMMERY. Her blood slopped round my ankles —

HOGBIN. Sufficient, was it? Two? I ask, that's all —

EPSOM. **What more is there?** (*Pause.*)

HOGBIN. What more? What more? Is imagination suffocated then? Is
anger drained? Is all possibility exhausted by four strokes?

EPSOM. We ain't sophisticated —

HOGBIN. No, but dream a little, you have dark yards of unthought
thought —

GUMMERY. Common soldiers, of the wars —

HOGBIN. Common, no! It is the likes of her have taught you commonness!
You have in you the seeds of every genius who ever walked, but unwatered,
no, don't, don't, it hurts to hear your nature stamped on, and by you...
(*Pause.*)

GUMMERY. I have axed seven Troys. What are you after?

HOGBIN. After?

GUMMERY. **Yer can't manipulate The People.**

HOGBIN. And would I try? Would I? I, scarcely shot of his virginity, new
to the razor, gauche, louche, cunt-mad, cunt-terrorized, swallower of
substances and kicker of cans, would I aspire to work one over you? You,
whose faces are bibles of experience, would I have the neck? (*Pause. They
admire him.*) Educated I may be, for all that means, and perceptive, yes,
gifted, I grant you, and with skills of certain sorts, Accountancy and the

European Mind, but arrogance, I'm spared, as you can see. (*He bows*.) All my wits are fagends, chipbags, and gutter dross beneath your boots... (*Pause*.)

EPSOM. Thank you.

HOGBIN. No more than your due.

EPSOM. He says so.

HOGBIN. I say so, and repeat as often as you fancy —

EPSOM. **And again!**

HOGBIN. I praise, I praise, but listen to what little judgement I have assembled, Helen's limbs are neither here nor there —

EPSOM. No, neither. Here nor there.

HOGBIN (*acknowledging*). You have the sticks, to you the wit — But Helen still rules Troy, the explanation of your unhappiness. (*Pause*.)

GUMMERY. What unhappiness?

EPSOM. 'ho are you calling un'appy? (HOGBIN *permits himself a smile*.)

HOGBIN. The unhappy, how slow they are to recognize themselves...! I say instead, unfulfilled. (*Pause*.) A jug half empty. An engine at low revs. An athlete with bound feet. I ask you, have you never thought you could do more?

EPSOM. You 'ave the echoing tones of an advert for a mother's tonic —

HOGBIN. **Well, yes, because great truth shares language with great error,** and luscious sunsets are reflected in slum windows... (*Pause*. HOGBIN *waits*.)

GUMMERY (*at last*). Yes...

EPSOM. Brian —

GUMMERY. **Yes, I said.** (*Pause*.) Because yes, who's happy? Don't say you are, Les, don't please, your fifteen pints are testimony to a desperate life —

EPSOM. **And your body.** (*Pause*.)

GUMMERY. My body? What of my body?

EPSOM. I've often thought, why is Brian so very — infatuated — with 'is body? A woman's, yes, that I cop, but to lavish such attention of yer own —

GUMMERY. **What in fuck's** —

EPSOM. Evidence of something, Brian —

GUMMERY. **What! What!**

HOGBIN. You see! You see, how once we look, we see! All points to our restlessness, and why? Because we know, we know, in every area, we are not whole... (*A profound pause*.)

GUMMERY (*looking around*). We'll say we couldn't find you... (*To* SAVAGE.) Could we? Couldn't find him? (*They go out*. HOGBIN *sinks to his knees, exhausted, ecstatic*.)

HOGBIN. Oh, wonderful, oh, luscious, **Gift of the gab.**

SAVAGE. I see your education was not wasted...

HOGBIN. All your seminars — **Shit on them** — all your critisism — **Piss on it** —

SAVAGE. Yes, yes —

HOGBIN. The Speak. The Speak! **The — Word — Saves — Life!** (EPSOM *comes back*.)

EPSOM. You do it.

HOGBIN (*horrified*). What?

EPSOM (*flinging a sickle, which slides over the floor*). What Helen needs. (*He goes out again.* HOGBIN *looks in horror at* SAVAGE. SAVAGE *lets out a laugh*.)

HOGBIN. Laugh. I love laughter. (*He laughs again*.) No, I love it. I do. Laugh. In the death camp. In the execution chamber. Balls to giggling, no, real laughter, please, the cosmic stuff, **Yer think I can't do it, cunt?** (SAVAGE *stops*.)

SAVAGE. I think it's easy. I think there is nothing easier in the world.

HOGBIN. **Flesh, what's that?**

SAVAGE. Quite.

HOGBIN. The jets come down, maim, maim! The rattle of the bofors, **Flesh, what's that?**

SAVAGE. You tell me.

HOGBIN. The stabbing on the Number 3. The wife carved in the basement. **Flesh, what's that?**

SAVAGE. Indeed...

HOGBIN. Two 'undred pounds of murder in the Mercedes boot, **Flesh, what's that!** (*Pause. He is kneeling on the floor with the weapon*.) Shove off, I 'ave to prepare myself... (*Pause*.)

SAVAGE. Will you tell Helen, or will I? (*Pause*.)

HOGBIN. Me.

SAVAGE. I'll send her, then?

HOGBIN. Yes. (SAVAGE *looks at him*.) Go on, then. (SAVAGE *withdraws. A great silence, attended by a movement of sky and light. At last* HOMER *appears, pushing* HELEN. *They stop*.)

HELEN. My boy. My only one. (HOGBIN *doesn't move*. SAVAGE *enters*. HOMER *goes to* HOGBIN, *who is dead. He looks at* SAVAGE.)

SAVAGE. **He refutes the argument.** And how? By counter-argument? Not Hogbin. No, Hogbin chooses to ignore. **No more quotation of the emaciated texts!** The testimony of experts, the beautifully laid bricks of theory, the towering cathedrals of logic, **not for him!** (*Pause*.) I wrote on his report, this student follows arguments, but lives by instinct, but which instinct, **Shame?** (*Pause*.) They'll put this down to love. But is it? (*He grabs* HOMER.) Is it? Is it love? (GAY *enters*. SAVAGE *releases* HOMER.)

GAY. Is my husband dead? (*They look at her*.) We were going to grow old together...! (*Pause*.) We were. When he had done his sentence. I would have waited at the prison door, holding the unloved blob. I would and he — (*To* SAVAGE.) Unforgivable, isn't it? **Unforgivable pessimism!** (*Pause*.) Which I have never suffered from and cannot for the life of me comprehend. (*She looks at him, feigning objectivity*.) Of course the only man I ever loved would choose to kill himself, that was as certain as night follows day, water runs downhill, etcetera, so why I, heaven knows why I — (*she begins caressing his body, kissing him, undressing him*) should be like this — at all — I can't — think — what — (*She moans*.)

HELEN. Gay.

GAY. When I — and — obviously — (*She sobs.*)

HELEN. Gay.

SAVAGE. Let her.

HELEN. Let her, why?

SAVAGE. Mourn —

HELEN. Mourn, why?

SAVAGE. **When Paris died you filled all Troy with mad woman's hollering!** (*She looks at him.*) And pints of your spit ran down the lintels, and your legs were bruised with kicking the inanimate, and servants ran from your flying pans of piss! (*To* HOMER.) He knows! He heard it!

HELEN. In those days I wept over every kind of trivia. (SAVAGE *stares at her.*) How you hate that. How you hate me to pulp the past and look on old fevers with contempt. What are you afraid of? Your coming neglect?

GAY (*rising to her feet*). Better now! (*She straightens her dress. To* HOMER.) Was he a hero? You know what heroes are.

SAVAGE. Coming neglect?

GAY. Heroes have reputations, and these reputations matter more than life itself. Is that correct?

SAVAGE. **What neglect?**

GAY. At crucial points the hero must choose between the death of reputation or death itself. Invariably he chooses —

SAVAGE. **I deny neglect's the consequence of passion —**

HELEN. Why? It happens.

SAVAGE. **I still deny.**

HELEN. Deny by all means —

GAY. **Will you be silent. I'm bereaved!** (*Pause.*)

HOMER. Helen, they will make you smaller still...

HELEN (*horrified*). Will they...? Oh, will they...? Have you seen...? (GUMMERY, EPSOM, OTHERS, *rush in.*)

GUMMERY. New Troy! Don't move, you unfulfilled!

EPSOM (*seeing the body*). Oi! (*He points.*) Accountant. Dead.

GUMMERY (*appalled*). Wholeness he promised me...

SAVAGE. Yes, but he was in a state of terror. Terror lent him speech.

GUMMERY. Wholeness...

SAVAGE. Speech of a reckless order —

GUMMERY. I long to be whole! (SAVAGE *is silent.*)

HELEN. Whole, yes, but whole for what? Health yes, but health for what? I am neither whole nor healthy and I am in torment if the wind blows from the East but have I ever asked for peace?

GUMMERY. Shut up.

HELEN. I ask you, peace for what? You must ask better questions —

GUMMERY. Shut up!

HELEN. Shh! Helen, not queen now, shh!

GUMMERY. How did he die?

SAVAGE. By choosing not to live.

GUMMERY. What was his name? Accountant, was it?

SAVAGE. He seemed content to be called Hogbin. I never heard him shun it.

GUMMERY (*hurt*). Hogbin? We can't have that. I prefer he be called — (*He is inspired.*) Hyacinth. (*He looks at him.*) I give up arms today. And punch nobody.

EPSOM. Brian —

GUMMERY. I give up knackering. And bruisery. I preach Hyacinth.

EPSOM. Brian —

GUMMERY. There are hyacinths all along the seashore. We waded through them, coming off the boats.

EPSOM. Remember it...

GUMMERY. **I preach him, then.** I, utterly illiterate, will preach, and where I falter, **praise my effort.** (*He braces himself.*) How much easier it was down the gym... (*Pause.*) Hyacinth says, great sunsets are reflected in slum windows. **I was such a window.**

EPSOM. Oh, fuck it, Brian —

GUMMERY. **I won't desist though speaking costs me blood.**

EPSOM. Daft bugger —

GUMMERY. Or grow wild with you, Les, however ill your criticism. Hyacinth would have me hear!

EPSOM (*indicating* HOGBIN'S *body*). Corpse of a yob!

GUMMERY. Throw away your liquor!

EPSOM. Bollocks.

GUMMERY. Tip away your beer!

EPSOM. Twice bollocks!

GUMMERY. I forgive this, Les —

EPSOM (*turning*). **You are a murderer.**

GUMMERY. Was, Les, was —

EPSOM. **And a woman butcher.**

GUMMERY. Was, was —

EPSOM. **And a child spitter.**

GUMMERY. Add to my list! Record not one, but every act of unfulfilment!

EPSOM. Unfulfilment? It was your finest hour!

GUMMERY. A slum window, reflecting every kind of filth, and you, on your rotting hinges, also reflect —

EPSOM. Don't call me a slum window —

GUMMERY. Oh, you catcher of bad lights! **Praise my powers and the body, shrivel!**

EPSOM. Goodbye, biceps...

GUMMERY. **Shrink!**

EPSOM. Pectorals, ta ta...

GUMMERY. Yes, muscles waste, because they flexed for evil. (*He waves his hand.*) That's it for today! (*He is breathless from exertion.*) I am tireder than I was from ninety press-ups, but I find myself, my unborn self...coming through the dark...

EPSOM. I shall miss you, my ol' mate...

GUMMERY (*wiping the perspiration off his face*). No, we shall —

EPSOM. No, we shan't —

GUMMERY. Seek you out and —

EPSOM. One day...one day... (*He goes out.*)

GUMMERY (*going to the cage*). Listen to me, did you? (*He laughs, shakes his head.*) No, we do change, we do... Make you a new cage...promise! (*He stretches wearily on the floor.*) To lie down...and know...what comes up behind me finds me...vulnerable...since I was a boy soldier, I always stood with my back to walls... (*He sleeps, vulnerably.*)

GAY. He's asleep.

HELEN. Oh, his little freedom... I could put his whole consciousness into my ear, and it would fit. Or up a fingernail, if I had fingernails... his entire knowledge would lie like greasy dirt between my toes...

GAY. Her arrogance... I do admire her arrogance, without admiring her at all...

HOMER. No one admires Helen. It is not admiration Helen wants. If I had made her admirable, who would know her name? (*He goes out.*)

SAVAGE. She is worn down. She is a butt. A scrag. She rubs out virtue **but the rubber also shrinks...**

GAY. How I detest you. The things you say to make your smoked-out lives seem purposeful!

SAVAGE. **My life is purposeful.** (HELEN *shrieks with a shrill laugh.*) Shriek, yes.

GAY (*goes to* HELEN). Oh, your dirty furrows...! I think of you two as fields deep in unrotted litter, ploughed and ploughed again and yielding less with every harvest **I am a perfectly beautiful and fertile woman** and I would not exchange one fallen hair for all your consciousness. (*Pause. She looks up.*)

HELEN. How you hate us.

GAY. Yes. Now someone cart my husband to the beach and let crabs chew his bits, this ten-day funeral nonsense was only an excuse for fucking, the widow got the males erect, I saw it, child between the laden tables, bewildered child, I saw it all —

HELEN. That's as it should be —

GAY. **Is it!**

HELEN. Yes, fuck the widow out of grief.

GAY. **You won't do anything proper.** (*Pause.*)

HELEN. I don't think we ever shall be reconciled. Neither time nor pain will bring us close.

GAY. Never. Your misdemeanours in Old Sparta were bad enough, but wickedness was fashion as long as there was order. There is no order any more. You're fifty and ridiculous.

HELEN. Oh, Helen, out of date!

GAY. Habitual **naughtiness.**

HELEN. What's worse than being out of date?

GAY. Fatuous **Mischief.**

HELEN. Armless and outmoded, god help me.

GAY. Where is the truth in you? Everything is **gesture!** (*Pause.*)

HELEN. Now, that's unfair —

GAY. Good, unfairness is our atmosphere! I hear my child calling, and though I hate it, I will give it milk. Obligation. Do you know the word?

HELEN. Yes. It's what we owe our feelings. (GAY *rushes to* HELEN, *seizing her head in her hands.*)

GAY. **Truncated and pontificating —**

HELEN. You are strangling me —

GAY. **Slut.** (*She detaches herself.*) You do — you really do — bring the violence out...in us... (*She goes out as* MACLUBY *and* FLADDER *enter with a cart.*)

SAVAGE. My student's dead.

MACLUBY. But not without his uses...

SAVAGE. I thought he'd learned a trick or two, but no, he's dead...

MACLUBY (*lifting the body onto the cart*). Dead in one sense.

SAVAGE (*looking at the body*). And once he jolted to cheap music...

MACLUBY. Persistent in another...

SAVAGE (*holding the dead youth's ankle*). His foot could not keep still — (*He shakes it.*) **Jive now!** Still now. **Throb now!** Still now. (*They begin to move away.*) Regret his death? No, a teacher must, a teacher worthy of the name, must welcome all the horror, such as — **Death calls in all our cavities** — And once he drummed his fingers in tutorials — (*He seizes* HOGBIN'S *hand.*) **Drum now!** Still now. **Twitch now!** Still now. But he emerged, he crawled from underneath the ruins of the rhythm, to know such things as — **Death calls in all our passages** (*They start to move.*) Don't go, don't go, let a man converse, eh? (*To* MACLUBY.) Regret his death, did you say, no, no, you see, he wanted through his fog, his pulsing fog, not knowledge but **Morality,** which I don't teach... (*They push the cart out.*) **Where are you taking him?**

BOY (*entering*). Hyacinth... (*He tosses a bar of soap to* SAVAGE. SAVAGE *catches it. Pause.*) New Troy of Cleanliness. (THE BOY *looks at his* FATHER, *then turns and follows the cart.*)

HELEN (*a sudden access of horror*). Do you love me??

SAVAGE. Are you afraid?

HELEN. **I said do you love me.**

SAVAGE. You are, you are afraid...!

HELEN. Say, then!

SAVAGE. Love? We have burst the word.... (*He looks after the departing cart.*) He looked at me and thought — I'm sure he thought — I could boil that... (*He smells the soap. Pause. He smells again. An expression of horror.*) **Hogbin! His very odour! Hogbin! His vest and socks!**

Interlude

A German archaeologist, circa 1902.

SCHLIEMANN. I came in search of Troy. I came in search of Helen's bed. Why? Because I am a European, and Europe begins in Helen's bed. But could I find Troy? I found Troy upon Troy upon Troy.

ASAFIR (*off*). Effendi! Effendi!

SCHLIEMANN. I hired labourers. I hired Anatolians, the finest diggers in the world. To see him dig! They talk of the coolie, but see the Turk!

ASAFIR. Effendi!

SCHLIEMANN. The Asiatics took Helen into Asia. The Europeans took Helen back again. At that moment they became a culture!

ASAFIR (*entering with an object*). Effendi...(THE LABOURER *thrusts the object at* SCHLIEMANN.)

SCHLIEMANN. Oh, Johnny, will you never learn? Dig, Johnny! (THE LABOURER *is disconsolate.*) The peasant does not discriminate between the spewings of industrial society and the most precious artefacts of the ancient world. **This is a bar of soap!** (*He hands it back to him.*) Please, bring me only good. *Nein gut, ja?* (ASAFIR *tosses the soap away.*) You could wash with that! Don't you want to wash? (*He goes out.*) These Troys, clustering upon real Troy, called themselves Trojans, but were they Trojan? Was Troy not dead?

YORAKIM. Effendi!

SCHLIEMANN. Desperate and ever-less viable imitations of a cultural entity expunged by history —

YORAKIM. Effendi!

SCHLIEMANN (*patiently*). The Turk, avaricious and notoriously cruel, is also a natural gentleman. In this, he astonishes us, who think of cruelty as alien to manners, what have we here? (YORAKIM *holds out a* A BABY *in a cloth. Pause.*) Are you trying to be funny? (YORAKIM *thrusts it at* SCHLIEMANN.) No, I do not wish to handle it. (*And again.*) Thank you, take it to its mother.

YORAKIM. No mother.

SCHLIEMANN Well, that's unfortunate. Did its mother die?

YORAKIM (*thrusting again*). **No mother.**

SCHLIEMANN. Then it must be taken to the Ottoman authorities. We are not an orphanage, we are an expedition.

YORAKIM (*pointing to the ground*). Dig! Dig!

SCHLIEMANN. Yes, good, dig until the light fails.

YORAKIM. **In dig.** (*Pause.*)

SCHLIEMANN. The child was in the dig? (YORAKIM *nods emphatically.*) Now, this is silly, how could it have been in — **It doesn't help for you to shout and wave, it does not help.** (*He uncovers* THE CHILD, *then sways with horror.*) Its arms are missing...! (*He thrusts it back at* YORAKIM.) What are you — what the — **You are trying to sabotage my mental stability** — it is hard enough to work in climates of this kind without — **I have never liked your face it is a screen of cunning** —

YORAKIM (*indignantly*). **In — dig.**

SCHLIEMANN. Liar! Asiatic liar!

YORAKIM. **No liar!** (*Pause.*)

SCHLIEMANN. What is a lie to you in any case? Scarcely a stain upon your soul, deceit is the weapon of the underdog, nothing can be credited where race rules race, but **I am an academic and truth is my** — (*Pause. He sways.*) All right, very well, thank you, this was bound to be a testing time, one cannot expect, seeking the bed, the seed and womb of Europe, can't expect, the womb of Helen being, no, you can't, and I certainly do not expect, so — (*Pause.*) Listen, my friend — (*Pause.*) No — you are not my friend, I apologize — listen, whoever you are, no baksheesh for baby, *nein*. (*He waves his hand.* YORAKIM *starts to leave, then suddenly stops, shouts.*)

YORAKIM. Effendi! (SCHLIEMANN *turns, alarmed.* YORAKIM *chucks the baby at him.* SCHLIEMANN *catches it, instinctively, as* YORAKIM *runs off.*)

SCHLIEMANN. **Aaaah!** (*He holds it at arms' length, in disgust. Darkness is falling. The sound of the evening prayer fills the stage as* THE LABOURERS *kneel towards Mecca.*) Your imperfection horrifies me...creeps along my wrists... (*Pause.*) Soon, so soon, the birth of monsters will be an impossibility, such will be the sprint of science...and all pain abolished...**You were born too soon.** (*He puts it on the ground.*) Even if my wife fell ill I could not sponge her face all day, I could not change her linen and remain a genius, it is a full time occupation, **You only come to me because I am a Christian**, but I also owe a duty to my soul. **I refuse to have my morality exploited!** (*He kicks the baby.*) **You exploit me!** (*Pause.*) Oh, God, am I one of your flock? (ASAFIR *appears, holding a sickle.*)

ASAFIR. Effendi!

SCHLIEMANN. The responsibilities of this ethic are too onerous, as Christ knew, and incompatible with freedom, **as Christ knew.**

ASAFIR. Effendi?

SCHLIEMANN (*looking at it*). I don't think, I really do not think this is of the least... (ASAFIR *jerks his head towards* THE CHILD) archaeological... (*He does the movement again.* SCHLIEMANN *sees.*) Oh, God, I do think the Turkish mind is of such extraordinary and shuddering cruelty... (ASAFIR *goes to* THE CHILD.) **How can you make carpets like you do?** (SCHLIEMANN *turns his back, resumes his lecture.*) These later Troys, clustering like — (*he hears the blow, lets out a stifled cry*) like — **There would be no knowledge if pity governed, would there, Asafir? You know.**

ASAFIR. Effendi?

SCHLIEMANN. You know. Look me in the eyes and say you know. Look me in the eyes, then... (*He takes him by the shoulder.*) ...stare in my European eyes with your Asiatic eyes, go on, stare, **stare...!** (ASAFIR *stares at the ground.*) Off now, Asafir, you casual murderer, you are already late for prayers...

ASAFIR. Baksheesh?

SCHLIEMANN. Baksheesh... (*Pause. He dips in his pocket.*) Baksheesh...

ACT THREE

Prologue

MACLUBY. The exhibitionists!
   No, they are though, to wreck our peace.
   Refuse to be wrecked
   I do
   I say
   Listen
   Copy me
   I say
   This is just another death I am singularly
   Unimpressed I look you in the eye whilst not
   Reducing one iota my walking pace
   Oh, you are cutting your throat
   Oh, you are dying on the steps
   Oh, I go,
   Fancy,
   And if the blood goes surging
   If it gushes down the cracks
   I lift my leg
   With
   Such
   Exquisite
   Grace
   No, you have to or they will **get our peace and**
   Bite it
   This suicide epidemic
   This madness epidemic
   And the beggars are a lake
   A lake of beggars
   A pond of suicides
   The rapids of the mad
   It takes some navigating the contemporary street
   But this is a revolution
   Who said
   This is a revolution
   Nobody told me
   I am a revolutionary also

Says the millionairess in the two-piece suit
And truth dripped through their jeers
In bloody clots

The weak brains pop
The frail imaginations pop
Like skulls in the boiler
Stalin
Who grew in wit as he grew in cruelty
Lenin
Who later on was rarely seen to smile
Robespierre
Gorky
Brecht
And all the strata smashers
All the rippers of the roots
They knew
That under pressure
They called it
The intensification of the struggle
Excellent
They called it
The growing strains of contradiction
I do love that
Under pressure
Our brains would pop
I hear it, ssh!
I hear it, ssh!
This also is a revolution, then
Nobody said
Oh, yes, a proper
I never knew
Shh!
The youth are popping
But they are always to the fore
Chucking bottles
Waving bayonets
Throwing matches at the poor
They are such ruthless imperialists of the soul
No
Let youth go
Bid youth farewell
Paris
Petrograd
Budapest
Warsaw
Europe's youth to the fore
To the workshops

Let us batter out a modern laugh
A laugh for the era
Not a boring howl
But something growing from the bowel
HAAAAA!
It's only the madwoman skating
Exquisitely skating on the suicide's gore

ACT THREE

Scene One

The gaol in Fragrant Troy. A place of baths and faucets.

HELEN. Where was the fat on him? Even his buttocks would have earned
a greyhound's pity...
SAVAGE. No fat...
HELEN. No fat, and yet boiled down he makes a million bars to perfume
Troy with...
GAOLER (*to* SAVAGE). Wash, you!
SAVAGE. I'm clean.
GAOLER. No one is clean.
SAVAGE. All right, but washed —
GAOLER. Wash again —
SAVAGE. It hurts my skin to wash it hourly —
GAOLER. The lather of Hyacinth brings only comfort to the sore —
SAVAGE. Yes, but —
GAOLER. Wash, then —
SAVAGE. Again?
GAOLER. Again. (*Pause.* SAVAGE *goes to the basin.*)
SAVAGE. I could go joyfully to a tramp's groin now —
GAOLER. And do it thoroughly
SAVAGE. Or suck great lungfuls from whores' cavities —
GAOLER. Front —
SAVAGE. Every crack would be a garden —
GAOLER. Back —
SAVAGE. The rank old human odour flooding the tortured nostril —
GAOLER. Now do her —
SAVAGE. Fart's paradise and sweat's apotheosis!
MACLUBY (*entering*). Today, you are fifty! (*He drapes a garland on him.*)
SAVAGE. Fifty...?
MACLUBY. And Helen fifty-five!
SAVAGE. But I was born in August!
MACLUBY. Why shouldn't dates be flexible! What's wisdom if it can't
burst calendars? What's a system if it can't call this the New Year One and
abolish stacks of squalid centuries?
SAVAGE. Let us out of here, we die of disinfectant...
MACLUBY. Fifty! An age without distinction! Fifty, and no solutions! (*To*
HELEN.) **Don't stare at his parts, Desire is soaped out of existence.**

SAVAGE. Fifty...?

MACLUBY. Fifty, and the ground shifting, fifty and the air thick with falling categories! It snows old faiths, it snows old dogmas! Fragrant Troy forgives your misdemeanours, how clean are you?

SAVAGE. Not clean yet...evidently...

MACLUBY. But washed? (*He sniffs him.*) You have the odour of the will to compromise, which is acceptable... (*He goes out.*)

HELEN. I have this horror we will never fuck again... (*Pause. SAVAGE is staring.*)

HELEN. I said I have this horror we will —

SAVAGE. Heard...

HELEN. Not because it is forbidden but because —

SAVAGE. Fifty...!

HELEN. You have lost the will — are you listening?

SAVAGE. **Fifty and no knowledge yet!** (*Pause. She stares appalled.*)

HELEN. No knowledge? Look at me. Sliced. Minimal. Reduced. Hacked. Slashed. Incapable. How dare you say no knowledge. **I am it.** (*Pause. He fixes her with a look.*) That isn't looking it's a fence.

SAVAGE. **What's a look, Helen?** (*Pause.*)

HELEN. What it is, I don't know. What is was, I will tell you. It was a thing as solid as a girder, down which streamed all the populations of our forbidden life... (*Pause. SAVAGE sobs.*)

CREUSA (*entering*). I have to tell you this. I am to be your wife again. (*They stare at her.*) Do you think I wanted it? (*Pause.*) **Well, speak, because you know it's possible.** Hatred could not prevent it. In that pit of contempt called bed we reached out sometimes like the drowning in the dark. **Even copulation we could do.**

HELEN. **Shut up.**

CREUSA. **It's possible and it happens in every place.** (*Pause.*) Clean Troy is to make divorce the only capital offence. And I, for all my maggot life am not ready to die just yet **We are to be a Show Marriage.** Life, yes, life in any mould, **speak then,** you must admire me above all martyrs, I am a martyr to nothing but life itself, and in the end **one male bit is much like any other** —

HELEN. **I vomit your** —

CREUSA. You would, you are a monument to pain —

HELEN. **Vomit your tolerance.** (*Pause.*)

CREUSA. The smell of Hyacinth...! In every bath and prison tub... Hyacinth, who could not make an entry while he lived, in tablet form swims through the lush of every woman's parts... (*To THE GAOLER.*) Let me out, please...! (*She goes. Pause.*)

HELEN. You did not deny. (*Pause.*) Did you? You did not deny? Or are my ears defunct in sympathy with other parts —

SAVAGE. I was so —

HELEN. Deny it then.

SAVAGE. Overthrown by —

HELEN. Indeed, but now —

SAVAGE. Disbelief —

HELEN. Now, though?

SAVAGE. Appalling and grotesque resuscitation of —

HELEN. So you won't —

SAVAGE. And yet it's possible. (*Pause. He looks at her.*) It's possible... (*He is aghast.*) Is it? (*Pause.*) **Horror!** (*Pause.*)

HELEN. I am indifferent who — with which bitch you — devour time — all skirt's your garden, out and plunge there by the armful, and if I discover you fat and naked in the compost, red from exploration, good but **No renunciation, please.** (*Pause.*)

SAVAGE. I am exhausted by —

HELEN. Yes —

SAVAGE. **The plunging lift of this infatuation.**

HELEN. It's not infatuation —

SAVAGE. Floor after floor of —

HELEN. **I have neither arms nor legs, it is not infatuation.** (*Pause.*)

SAVAGE. I think...let me speak...I think...you are a barrier to knowledge now, when once you were the absolute condition... (*Pause.*)

HELEN. All my life I was afraid I might recant, but never did. Always, it was the man who suffocated passion in the puddle. (*Pause.*) Don't be the grey-arsed priest, I beg of you, don't hide under the arch, squatting on your heels and with a withered finger trace the ancient hieroglyphs, all intellect and sterile. Let me be the board you chalk your meaning on, chalk screaming on the wet slate of my wounds... (*He doesn't respond.*) All right, renounce... (*Pause.*)

SAVAGE. Helen —

HELEN. No, shh, all words suddenly redundant —

SAVAGE. Helen —

HELEN. Can't hear you —

SAVAGE. I have to know what —

HELEN. Words, aren't they weapons? Aren't they wires? Keep your weapons off me! Look out, wires!

SAVAGE. **Renunciation also must be knowledge.** (*Pause.*)

HELEN. I don't persuade. I never have persuaded. They persuaded me. Helen never urged a man, he came, he drenched her in his fever, (*with a sudden wail*) oh, undress me, no one's looking, I am maimed without you, and fuck all limbs, this is the torture...! (*He stares at her.*) What have you learned, then? That you hate Helen?

SAVAGE. Yes —

HELEN. Hate her, and could punch the sight out of her eyes —

SAVAGE. Yes —

HELEN. The feeling out of her lips —

SAVAGE. **All right...!**

GAOLER (*entering*). Go home, now, citizens...

HELEN. **Oh, the gross intrusion of banality...**

GAOLER. Thank you, and take your bowls —

HELEN. Persist...

GAOLER. Towels to the laundry —

HELEN. Persist...! (*The infusion of the city.*)

Scene Two

A Public Place. The cage is no longer visible. FLADDER *enters holding a gong and sits.*

GAY (*entering*). The Concentrated Thoughts of a Great King Deposed, Reviled, Neglected and Eventually Rehabilitated in the Interests of Universal Harmony! (*To* FLADDER.) Beat the gong if you deny my version. (*He gongs.*) Not yet, silly. (*Pause.*) My catastrophic marriage to a — (*He gongs.*) No, let me get started, gong at the end if you have to. (*She composes herself.*) My catastrophic marriage to a libidinous woman inexorably led to the death of thousands — (*He gongs.*) How can you gong that? Everybody knows that! It's a Historical Fact. If you are going to gong everything we will take the gong away from you. You abuse the privilege of age. (*She proceeds.*) When I was destitute I came to truth — (*He gongs.*) Give it to me! (*She snatches it and tosses it offstage.*) **You are trying to ridicule the Government of Fragrant Troy** — (*He shakes his head.*) You are and we are not obliged to tolerate it! (*She rehearses.*) In poverty I discovered twenty truths —
One! In limitation lies the source of satisfaction.
Two! The question leads only to the next question.
Three! You have to die some time.
Four! The final end of equality is universal plastic surgery. (FLADDER *makes a noise in his throat.*) Shut up —
Five! To suffer is to be without soap! (*He gurgles.*) Shut up, I said —
Six! Dig your garden till the sun sets.
Seven! And when the soldiers have gone, plant it again.
Eight! (*To* FLADDER.) **I shall not desist, no matter how you gurgle.** (*Pause.*)
Eight! If you must kiss do it with your eyes open.
Nine! The greatest joy is to concede.
Ten! Don't grieve after midnight
Eleven! (*To* FLADDER, *who is frothing.*) **This is what you discovered, isn't it? Keep still, then.** (*Pause.*) Eleven! Fornication is the aptitude of mongrels.
Twelve! Swans mate for life.
Thirteen! Violence is no solution.
Fourteen! Nor is justice.
Fifteen! Soap is experience. (*To* FLADDER.) **You are dribbling on my leg.**
Sixteen! (*Pause.*) Sixteen! (*To* FLADDER.) **You see, I am not sabotaged by you!** (*Pause.*) Sixteen! The majority are sometimes right.
Seventeen! It is perfectly natural to hate.
Eighteen! It is love that's artificial.
Nineteen! Marriage is the government. (*To* FLADDER.) **No, I won't stop!**

Twenty! (*Pause.*) Twenty! (*Pause.*) The Past never occurred! (*She pushes him off his knees.*) I did it! I did it, and I was not stopped by you!. (*Pause. She looks at him.*) What does it matter if you thought those things or not? What does it matter ? Clean Troy is not about truth. It's about me. Now, get off your knees and scarper. (*He climbs to his feet.*) Take your gong. (*He moves.*) Do you still love my mother? (*He stops.*) You do...You do love her...! (*Pause. She looks closely into him.*) Is there anything she could do — anything — would stop you loving her? (*Pause.*) Extraordinary. (*She walks a little, still looking at him.*) I once put corpses in her bed. Arms and things. By this I meant to say, this wrist, this bowel, you caused to howl, you caused to wither. But she was only irritated by the smell. Is that the reason for her power? (HOMER *enters, senile now, and with two sticks.*)

HOMER. Please, don't let them bath me again...

GAY. You must be bathed!

HOMER. Not so often, surely?

GAY. Yes, often and often! Do they scrub you?

HOMER. Yes!

GAY. That's good, I told them, scrub him in every crack and pore because that's where his misery collects, and his misery makes him sing those songs, oh, so miserable your songs are now, and anyone who hears you, they get miserable too! Why did Odysseus go back to Penelope? (HOMER *stares, bewildered.*) I asked you a question. I mean, hadn't he met this girl, this perfect girl? So why did he go back to Penelope? **She must have been a proper hag by then.** (*Pause.*)

HOMER. No more soap!

GAY. Oh, take him away and wash him...

HOMER. No more soap!

GAY (*turning on him*). **I think you must defend your fictions and not take that arrogant stance.**

HOMER (*as he is hurried out*). Oh, God, not soap...!

GAY (*to* CREUSA, *who enters with* SAVAGE). I don't believe he has the slightest interest in art any more. He is interested in soap, and only soap. (*She smiles.*) Now, are you reconciled? You must consummate the marriage, and in public. And to think we once had public executions! No, this is progress —

CREUSA. I wonder if I can —

GAY. Please, don't throw up objections...! How girlish you are...!

CREUSA. Yes...

GAY. When you have been so — used — and flogged — and flung around like soldiers' baggage... (*She kisses* CREUSA *on the cheek.*) Your cheeks are maps of sordid life... (CREUSA *goes out.* GAY *watches her.*) The Troys are slipping away. So many errors...your sacrifice is a small thing compared to our survival.

SAVAGE. Sacrifice? I could not do it if it were a sacrifice.

GAY. What is it, then?

SAVAGE. An education, obviously.

GAY. I might also be an education... (*Darkness falls on the stage.*)

SAVAGE. On Monday I washed the body of the old woman.

On Tuesday I cut the throat of a stranger.
On Wednesday I lifted potatoes from the allotment.
On Thursday I seduced the mother of my lover.
On Friday I was ashamed and unable to act.
On Saturday I read the works of great authors.
On Sunday I lay and wished I was a baby.
On Monday...
On Monday I washed the body of the old woman...

GAY. I'll take my clothes off, shall I?

SAVAGE. It's night...!

GAY. I will, if you will...

SAVAGE. The dictator stirs inside his bunker...

GAY (*removing her shoes*). Shoes first...

SAVAGE. The executioners are checking their weapons...

GAY. Then socks...

SAVAGE. And intellectuals rip the membranes of humanity in their shuddering cots... **All right, undress!** (*Pause.*)

GAY. If I am naked and you are not, what then? (SAVAGE *shakes his head.*) One of us has the advantage, but who...?

SAVAGE. You ask questions like a man throws stones. You talk to fend off silence.

GAY. I have the advantage! (*She flings off her last garment. She stands naked. Pause.*) Stare at me, then. (*Pause.*) Stare. (*Pause.*) Consume me. (*Pause.*) Are you consuming me? (*Pause.*) You're not, are you? Or are you, I can't tell from — (*She sees* FLADDER, *sitting.*) Oh, God, there is a man still here! (*She covers herself with her hands.*)

SAVAGE. What's the matter? He can't speak.

GAY. He can see me — he — **sees me.**

SAVAGE. But what he sees he can't put into words. So what he sees he sees as the stars see. Or the stones. Do you hide yourself from stones? (*Pause.*)

GAY. If you do not respond to me, I shall be damaged. I shall be damaged and the onus will be on you! (*Pause. Suddenly she goes to grab her clothes but* SAVAGE *seizes them first.*)

SAVAGE. You look ridiculous. Beautiful and ridiculous. (*She goes to snatch them but he whips them away. She looks, uncomprehending. She attempts to smile.*)

GAY. What's this? Desire?

SAVAGE. **Desire!** Do you think beauty makes desire? Do you think you only need to **stand and be observed?** (*She looks alarmed.*) It's night... (*She looks nervously to* FLADDER.) Don't look to him. He is a stone.

GAY. Are you going to — **cut me into bits?** (*Pause. He is bemused. He sinks to the ground. Extends a hand limply.*)

SAVAGE. Shh...

GAY (*horrified*). **Are you?**

SAVAGE. Shh... (*He shakes his head.*) Oh, pitiful...oh, unknowing... (*He beckons her with a gesture. Timidly she goes to him. He encloses her chastely in his arms. A figure enters from the darkness. It is* GUMMERY, *carrying* SHADE *in a small cage at his belt. He looks at* GAY. *He looks at* SAVAGE.)

GUMMERY. No anger but. (*Pause.*) I walk along the shore so full of kindness for the world. (*Pause.*) No anger but. (*Pause.*) We have our nightly stretch so kindness-sodden and we see his widow and our queen. No anger, obviously. Undressed. (*Pause.*) Much as old Helen might have been. (*Pause.*) Kindness is bruised and Hyacinth demeaned... (*He turns to go, stops.*) How hurt we are. No anger but. (*He starts to leave*).

SAVAGE. How hideous you are. Without your anger. How crippled and deformed. So kind you make all kindness loathsome not that it seemed a very precious thing but now it stinks the corpse of undone actions all tumours in your lung you passive and colourless licker of fallacies I see when I look at you why heroes have to die, Homer was right in this at least he did not pursue the Greeks to their retirement, shuffle, stagger away you offend the landscape and my vocabulary withers in describing you, I, a doctor, too. Speechless, and in revulsion... (GUMMERY *is terribly still.*) Cart your shrunk mate off, you spoil a decent night. (GUMMERY *remains.*) And yet you stay. To test what, I wonder? (GUMMERY *is still.* SAVAGE *climbs to his feet.*)

GUMMERY. Once, I made my body iron. To hurt. And now it's iron to suffer... (*Pause.*)

SAVAGE. Suffer? For what? My student's gabble? There was panic in his trousers.

GUMMERY. **Test me.**

SAVAGE. And you were cruel...they told me... (SAVAGE *goes to* GUMMERY, *who is still motionless. He stands behind him.*)

GAY (*suddenly*). **Can't watch!** (*She grabs her clothing, runs to* FLADDER.) **Can you?** (*She rushes out.*) **Can't watch!** (*Wind. Darkness. The peculiar voice of* SHADE, *tunefully.*)

SHADE. Intellectuals also kill! Intellectuals kill!
Intellectuals also kill! Intellectuals kill!

Scene Three

Bells. MACLUBY *besuited.* CREUSA *gowned. They look over the city.*

MACLUBY. Troy isn't what it was, when you last wed.

CREUSA. Nor Creusa, either.

MACLUBY. Troys have been, and Troys have gone...

CREUSA. And Creusas, they have been and gone, too...

MACLUBY (*smiling*). This is the proper spirit for matrimony.

CREUSA. Yes.

MACLUBY. Accommodation.

CREUSA. Yes.

MACLUBY. No more climbing the greasy pole of personality, but —

CREUSA. Yes. Because I fell, and fell, and fell again... (*A blast of rattles and cheers as a massive bed descends. It is upholstered with twig or flint.)* **What's that...!**

MACLUBY. No one said it would be easy...

GAY *(entering)*. The territory of epic adventures! The poor man's empire! I am a romantic, at least I have kept that alive! *(To* CREUSA.) On the bed now, and good luck in the maze! I think it is a maze, with its dead ends and repetitions, but at the centre of which is — must be — for those who persevere — I don't know what! (CREUSA *is helped to the bed. Crowd applause.*) How Troy needed this! Listen! When all was disintegration and morals were exploding nebulae! The young particularly will appreciate this **Affirmation,** hurry, make yourself comfortable, your husband is **imminent.** (CREUSA *lies on the bed.*) This shows as nothing better can, the utter **Circularity of life,** the fact we teach in school that if you walk defiantly away from a fixed point, the earth's roundness ensures you will return to that same spot, no matter how terrible the journey! **The loop of knowledge.** He's coming! *(Whistles.)* I could weep with that strange weeping women do at weddings! I could! (SAVAGE *enters, in a motheaten and devastated suit. Applause. She looks at him. She kisses him chastely of the cheek. He stares at the spectacle of the bed. Silence falls.*)

SAVAGE. It's twigs...

CREUSA. Not as bad as you might —

SAVAGE. It's twigs...!

MACLUBY. Climb in, Dr Savage...

SAVAGE *(a terrible connection)*. **It's a pyre!**

MACLUBY. You are the one who wants the knowledge —

SAVAGE. **A pyre when I'm not dead...!**

CREUSA. All right, all right...

SAVAGE. **Not dead...**

CREUSA. Shh...shh... *(He mounts the bed. He sits rigidly and apart from her. The occasional rattle from* THE CROWD.)

MACLUBY. And Odysseus went to Penelope, and slew her suitors, and having washed the blood from his hands, undressed her, and she undressed him, and as she did, his eyes travelled her worn and imperfect body, and her eyes saw his decay, and they wept, and pity was the source of his tumescence... what else could it have been?

CREUSA. Look at me with new eyes, or we shan't do it...

SAVAGE. I can't.

CREUSA. It can be done...

SAVAGE. Anything can be done, but not with new eyes...

CREUSA. Hold my hand, then —

SAVAGE. Trying —

CREUSA. Hold it — *(She extends hers.* THE CROWD *whistles and claps.)* **Hold it...** *(With a spasm of pain,* SAVAGE *thrusts his hand into hers. More applause.)* It's all right...! It's all right...!

MACLUBY. The Political Fuck! Not for the first time, the Political Fuck! *(As* THE CROWD *chants its approval,* HELEN *appears pushed by* HOMER.)

HELEN. What can you see?

HOMER. You've got the eyes, not me —

HELEN. To the left!

HOMER. Some agony —

HELEN. The right then! (THE CROWD *obscures her view.*) Oh, shift you fragrant lawyers!

MACLUBY (*watching* SAVAGE'S *agony*). He squirms, he sweats, but that's the pain a rebirth brings, if birth was painless, would a child be loved?

HOMER. What do you see?

HELEN (*straining*). A bed —

HOMER. A bed —

HELEN. A terrible bed...

MACLUBY. This is the union from which all stale and mothy marriages will suck their consolation!

GAY (*like a trainer*). Kiss him, kiss him, do! **More lamps, they are obscure!** (*Spotlights heat the bed.*) The lips release the tongue, the tongue unlocks the fingers, the fingers free the fastenings, the fastenings ungate the flesh, oh, claim her, do...! (*With a desperate effort of will,* SAVAGE *flings himself on* CREUSA. THE CROWD *surges as the bed is drawn out of sight.*)

MACLUBY (*laughing*). Knowledge...! Knowledge...!

HELEN. Oh, my own madman, does he grin or weep...?

Scene Four

HELEN *is alone,* SHADE'S *cage at her feet.* THE BOY *enters, no longer a boy.*

BOY. My father and my mother have been reconciled. And in spite of her advancing years, she has conceived. They are calling it a miracle.

HELEN. Miracles happen when desire's dead...

BOY. My father wanted me to be an intellectual, but I lean towards business. (*Pause.*)

HELEN. You are the soap maker.

BOY. I wash out minds as well... (*He peers into the cage.*) Is there meant to be a bird in here?

HELEN. Yes. He sings all day long.

BOY. Can't hear him.

HELEN. Really? I find him deafening. Why are you dressed like an undertaker?

BOY. An undertaker? No one has ever said that before. I think of myself as a bridegroom. May I tell you about soap? It is my obsession.

HELEN. How lucky you are to have an obsession. And you can't be more than thirty-two.

BOY. Oh, dear, I think you are going to interrupt me all the time.

HELEN. Isn't that allowed?

BOY. It breaks the flow.

HELEN. I don't like flows. The best things can be said staccato.

BOY. Nevertheless, I will persist.

HELEN. How can I avoid you? My nurse is old and falls asleep, and it's not as though an amputee has anything to block her ears with —

BOY. I came to soap thinking it a product —

HELEN. You would not believe the sheer variety of human innocence that foists itself on me! Poets, infertile women, men with agony inside their trousers, I have to tolerate the lot —

BOY. But it is not a product, it is a culture. For example —

HELEN (*conceding*). **All right, flow.** (*Pause.*)

BOY. There has never yet been a society that could tolerate the smell of human flesh, can you explain that? The individuals who live with most intensity the odour of mankind have always been the outcasts, the vagrant, the dispossessed. We are born with a profound revulsion for our own scent, an antipathy formed during some nightmare travel down the birth canal — I speculate — but certainly the odour of the mass can turn the stomach and I believe the essence of the human smell to be a lethal toxin. This is soap's justification and the fulcrum of an honourable career. (*He smiles.*) But my concentration on the subject led me further, as indeed all concentration will, no matter how banal the subject. The great banker also knows the human heart. So soap revealed its laws to me. (*Pause.*) Your eyes are shut but you hear everything, I know —

HELEN. You have his voice, but without the edge of panic that clung to all his vowels...

BOY. My flow, please... (*Pause.*) Soap makes harmony, and made with proper inspiration, lets imagination compensate for impossibly demanding life. Which brings me to my point, that you might understand the need for what I hope to call Essential Helen, as Hogbin's body, all kindness and purity, pervades the Trojan spirit now. (*Pause.*) Respond, by all means. (*She is silent.*) Sometimes the horror of an idea is only the boom of its essential truth... (*Pause.*) And now you won't talk...! (*Pause.*) We see in your life spectacularly the price of Eros. I don't stoop to criticize, but simply draw to your attention the fifteen thousand orphans of the Peloponnese, the wail of widows and wounds of conscripts whose total ache would lift the mountains off their feet, I am not judging, you understand I am not ethical, the children of these wars eat murder with their breakfast. I don't judge.

HELEN. What you describe is consequence. I refuse the blame. Every conscript had his choice and every widow could have blocked her man. But if they died for Eros, where's the tragedy in that? In other wars they'll scream for flags, sometimes for banks, or even books, I've heard. No, cunt's a worthy cause as slaughters go.

BOY. You grab the argument! Beauty has this effect, it stirs the blood, and yes, it is a truth of sorts.

HELEN. Truth...? Oh, don't drag truth in, I'm over sixty —

BOY. Very well, but whether it's a truth or not, it cannot be a lie —

HELEN. Beauty is a lie! Of course it is a lie! (*He shrugs.*) It is simply the best available lie on the subject of truth... (*Pause. He smiles, shaking his head.*)

BOY. My flow... my flow... (*Pause.*) But I proceed. However great the pain
　　your Eros brought, we cannot dispense with Eros. It lives in all of us. It
　　cries, and breathes.

HELEN. In you? It cries, and breathes?

BOY (*charmingly*). Now, that is sabotage —

HELEN. Preposterous claim —

BOY. All right, it cries in varying degrees, but because I don't stand out at
　　passing skirt is no —

HELEN. He must defend his sprig!

BOY. Really, you will not disorganize me by —

HELEN. I won't disorganize him —

BOY. By some phallic contest which —

HELEN. He's not disorganized —

BOY. Is both grotesque, pernicious and —

HELEN. He's not, he's definitely not disorganized —

BOY. No —

HELEN. And I don't want to disorganize you, God knows the mayhem if
　　you were, I shrink to think, the uncaging of, the swollen veins, no, no, you
　　stay as you are! (*Pause.*)

BOY (*coolly*). You are piqued.

HELEN. The flow, for pity's sake.

BOY. You are piqued and I know why.

HELEN. Me? Helen? Piqued?

BOY. Because I look at you with cool and level eyes. (*Pause.*)

HELEN. You do. I grant you that.

BOY. Which you are unaccustomed to.

HELEN (*pause. Then with inspiration*). The story of the Actress in the
　　Penal Colony! The star who had made a million men throb in the stalls
　　found the interrogator unyielding and her breasts showing though the
　　dirty quilted jacket moved his lust his pity his ambition **not one bit** so solid
　　and so thick the plating of his **ideology,** and this made her weep. But when
　　she had been returned to the cells he locked his door and stropped
　　himself. **At that moment the soul of The Party died.** (*Pause.*) You are so
　　oblique and so well-mannered, a proper skater, as black as a fly and im-
　　possible to swat. A man for the age. Why do you want my body?

BOY. To give all women, so all women may be, at moments of their choice,
　　Hellenic... (*A terrible howl comes from HELEN.*) You howl — yes — you
　　howl but —

HELEN. **My — opic Per — fumier!**

BOY. The lending of transgression to the ashamed, the loan of passion to the
　　guilty, the licensing of total love to the domestic —

HELEN. **Fastidious sycophant!**

BOY. **You don't like people —**

HELEN. No —

BOY. You scorn their simple pleasures, you mock the scale of their imagin-
　　ation —

HELEN. Yes, every day!

BOY. **It's unforgivable!** (*Pause.*)

HELEN. Could I ever forgive myself if I were forgivable? (*Pause. He looks at her.*)

BOY. Your lonely and malevolent life... (*Pause.*) We terribly want to help you —

HELEN. Afraid —

BOY. Who —

HELEN. You. Afraid.

BOY. Afraid, of what?

HELEN. Afraid I'll cling in the imagination of a girl, or in a boy's head, make all his thoughts unscholarly... (*Pause.*)

BOY. Helen — if I may call you Helen —

HELEN. Well, don't call me anything else —

BOY. Helen —

HELEN. That's it, though you say it oddly —

BOY. You have not seen yourself for years.

HELEN. No. I have no mirror.

BOY. I think, if you were to — examine your appearance — you might understand that your capacity for mischief is now, sadly —

HELEN. You talk like a shrivelled priest, and the language shrivels when you talk it — do you mean I'm ugly? I was born ugly. You think that slipping and sliding word circumscribes my power? You're not — though a lipstick maker and a skin-cream bottler — so bereft of knowledge as all that, surely? (*Pause.*) No, you cannot have my fat to let unsuffering women play at deepest life...better the crabs get dinner off me... (*He goes out.* FLADDER *comes in, carrying the gong.*) They want to smear themselves with essence, the new Trojans. Think with a soap called Helen they might temporarily contract desire. Sign nothing. And when I'm gone, in the sea with the remnants, they will boil me otherwise and use my fat to humiliate some unborn class... (*Pause.*) Tell me, is it possible for Helen to be old? (*He gongs. Pause.* A CHILD *enters, without arms.*) Oh, look, she has in her the same appalling gift...! (HELEN *grins.*) It's in her hip...the tilting of her head...**Oh, the wreck of domesticity and the tearing of men from regular employment...!**

CHARITY. What?

HELEN. Shh! Your mother!

CHARITY. Tear men from regular employment? How?

HELEN. It can't be told, it happens!

GAY (*entering*). Listen! The Festival of Families! And we'll be late! (THE CHILD *runs off.* GAY *follows, then stops.*) May I kiss you?

HELEN. Kiss me...?

HELEN. Yes. (*Pause, then* GAY *kisses her, goes out. Pause.*)

HELEN (*apprehensively*). I think I am going to be killed. (*Pause.*) Beat the gong, then... (*Pause.*) So they are killing me, **Who is.** (*Pause.*) You know and you're not telling me! (*Pause.*) **Who is.** (*Pause.*) You? (*Pause.*) Well, why not you? Because it isn't in your character? **What is your character?** To think any one of us is knowable, when personality is only crystal grinding between stones, **don't come near me yet.** (*He is still.*) I want to be killed. But in a gush of violence. I wanted to be beaten out of life by some mad male all red about the neck and veins outstanding like the protesting prostitute in the bite of the night, discovered all brain and sheet and stocking **Not this cold political thing,** hacked to shreds among the bedthings **Not this,** the wonderful gore that trickled underneath the door, **Not this though!** (*Pause. He is still.*) Who signed the warrant? (*She looks at him.*) **The entire population did?** Oh, come on, even the children? **And the as yet unborn?** (SAVAGE *enters, stops. She glimpses him.*) Don't come near. I would rather be blind than see you again. Oh, suddenly the air is thick with stale longings, and sweats gone acid with betrayal, **Old husband and old lover,** I would prefer to be slashed by a passing killer than you two set about me kindly, considerate in strangling, considerate in suffocating, **The considerate lover was always the worst** — (SAVAGE *makes a move.*) **Don't come into my eyeline, I would ram my sight out rather on a branch!** (*He freezes. She averts her face.*) Oh, this purgatory of flowerbeds, in Old Troy temper was the rule, I don't belong and — **Where's Homer!** (*Pause.*) Oh, my maker's gone... Someone has extinguished him...what for? **A poet's soap?** (*She looks at* SAVAGE.) It must have been you...what was it? Did his weeping anger you? We do feel bitter, don't we, towards the genius whose final statements are so trite? But he was silent at the end...the sight of me...robbed him of speech... Whereas you...are shameless...which I loved... (EPSOM *enters, with a cloth. She sees him, from the corner of her eye.*) The knacker comes. (*She grins.*) One for the soap yard!

EPSOM. Got a job to do...

HELEN. A job, he calls it! Magnificent monster! And for a terrible hour I thought there was no one left who hadn't changed!

EPSOM. Change, for what?

HELEN. For what! Exactly! Look at him, as unredeemed as when a dirty boy he worked his snot between his tutor's teeth...(*Pause.* EPSOM *goes to* HELEN.)

EPSOM (*intimately*). Be yer mate...

HELEN (*not grasping his meaning*). Why not be my mate! What's a little strangulation between friends? I have seen torturers play chess with their victims, and the mothers of drowned infants fuck the perpetrators, no, it's all right, it is! (*He goes to cover her.*) **Sav — age!** (*Pause.*) Can you watch this? (*Pause.*) You can. You can watch this... (EPSOM *silences her by dropping the cloth over her face. Silence. He puts his hands about her throat. He exerts. He stops. Pause.*) No, that's wrong, surely... (*He grimaces, as if at effort.*) The way you handle my neck, Les, I've been loved better —

EPSOM. Die! (*He exerts.*)

HELEN. Yes, I long to, but —

EPSOM. Die! (*A pause, her head drops forward. An immediate cacophony of factory whistles.*)

FLADDER. The revolutionaries are flunkeys, too! The terrorists transport dominion in their handshakes!
We know but we still act!
We know but we still act! (EPSOM *drives away* THE AUDIENCE *which has gathered at the scene.* FLADDER *runs out.*)

EPSOM. Fuck off! Scarper! (A WOMAN *is going near* THE BODY.) Off, yer vermin!

WOMAN. Cures tumours, whore's blood!

EPSOM. No, it's 'angman's spit yer thinkin' of! (*He gobs at her. She flees. He laughs. Others risk his blows to touch* HELEN *for luck, and run.*)

SAVAGE. I can watch. I can watch anything.

EPSOM. It's a gift, mate... (THE PUBLIC *are repulsed by* EPSOM.)

SAVAGE. I think to believe in every lie is better than to see through every truth...

EPSOM (*fetching a broom*). Sweeping up...

SAVAGE (*draws near* HELEN). In passion, the woman births the man. The convulsions of her flesh are births...

EPSOM (*sweeping*). I wouldn't know...**Clear of the body, please!**

SAVAGE. Imagine, then.

EPSOM. Who, me?

SAVAGE. Why not you? (EPSOM *shrugs*.) **I insist that you imagine.** (EPSOM *stops sweeping*.) To have had Helen, imagine it...

EPSOM. Trying...

SAVAGE. Yes, but to have had Helen, and to have no longer, **Imagine that.** (EPSOM *shrugs*.) The greater the love, the more terrible the knowledge of its absence. No sooner did she love me than I longed for her death, **And you call yourself a monster!** (*Pause*.)

EPSOM. I think —

SAVAGE. Yes!

EPSOM. I think —

SAVAGE. **I am what you are only in your dreams.** (*He goes to* HELEN, *and takes her in his arms*.)

EPSOM (*horrified*). **Clear of the body!**

SAVAGE. Down the tunnels of her ears, I whisper... (*He mutters*.) Down the chasm of her throat I murmur... (*He draws the cloth from her mouth and kisses her*.)

EPSOM. **All right...!** (SAVAGE *lets the cloth fall, goes out. Pause. Then* EPSOM *goes to* HELEN *and removes the cloth. Pause*.)

HELEN. Not dead...

   Until he spoke...

   Not dead...

   Why not, bastard...!

EPSOM. Search me —

HELEN. Any death I would have welcomed and you spare me to hear that!

EPSOM. I thought —

HELEN. What was it, pity?

EPSOM. I suppose —

HELEN. Pity...!

EPSOM. I take life and I'm criticized, I give life and I'm criticized, **can't I pity sometimes, too?**

HELEN. Oh, utter decline...Helen pitied...And I thought...for a moment...I dared think you had spared me for lust... (*She laughs*.)

Scene Five

CREUSA *comes in, an old woman pregnant.* SAVAGE *is alone.*

SAVAGE. It's time. (*Pause.*) It's time to write the book.

CREUSA. On what? Soap wrappers?

SAVAGE. Your interventions were always so mundane.

CREUSA. There is so little paper here and one time it was blowing down the gutters, wrapped around the lamp-posts, fine cartridge, too, but who remembers Paper Troy? Collect today for tomorrow may be barren! As for pencils...!

SAVAGE. Can't write the book, then...

CREUSA. And reading's out of date...

SAVAGE (*relieved*). Can't write the book... (*She shrugs, sits on a stool.*) Inevitable. The greatest document fails to exist. (CHARITY *hurries in.*)

CHARITY. Skipped Hygiene! Skipped Good Citizens and Family Love! Don't tell! (*She is about to run out.*)

SAVAGE. Seen a bit of paper?

CHARITY. Paper? What's that?

CREUSA. You see...!

CHARITY. Oh, that stuff the soap comes in?

SAVAGE (*grinning*). **Can't write the book!**

CHARITY. Write a book? What for?

SAVAGE. To spread unhappiness, of course...

CHARITY (*inspiration*). I'll be the book. They say that men in concentration camps learned poems of nine thousand lines. I can do that! (*She sits cross-legged.*) Ready! (*She gets comfortable.*) Now, you speak!

GAY (*entering with officers*). You say you saw it happen —

FIRST OFFICER. Everybody did —

GAY. Where is she, then?

FIRST OFFICER. **I repeat we all saw Helen die.**

GAY. All legless and armless women, fetch them in!

SECOND OFFICER. There's only one in all of Troy -

GAY. Bring her! (THE OFFICER *leaves.*) They say that Helen's dead —

SAVAGE. She is. I kissed her cooling mouth.

GAY. Then where's the body?

CHARITY. **We're trying to write a book!**

GAY. Be quiet you precocious little — and I can see your knickers, you are not to sit like that!

CREUSA. You were the same —

GAY. I was never —

CREUSA. You were just the —

GAY. **It is not possible I was like that.** (CREUSA *shrugs.* THE OFFICER *pushes in* A POOR WOMAN *on a trolley. She is armless and legless.*)

SECOND OFFICER. Do you mean this?

GAY. Yes. How did she lose her limbs?

SECOND OFFICER. She fell under a tram. To be precise, she fell under two.

GAY. When?

OFFICER. When —

GAY. Not you. (*To* WOMAN.) You.

OLD WOMAN. When there were trams, of course.

GAY. She's lying. When were there ever trams?

FIRST OFFICER. During Mechanical Troy.

GAY. Mechanical Troy... I'd forgotten Mechanical Troy.

FIRST OFFICER. It rusts in shady corners...

GAY (*to* THE WOMAN). Well, if you'd lived in Dancing Troy, you'd only have got bad feet.

OLD WOMAN (*creaking with laughter*). Seen some of 'em! I prefer me truck.

GAY. This can't be Helen, she's far too sensible.

SECOND OFFICER (*to* THE WOMAN). Shove off! (*They start to leave.*)

GAY. Wait a minute! (*She stops.*) Which tram?

OLD WOMAN. The 3.

GAY. In which direction?

OLD WOMAN. Empty. To the Depot. (*Pause.*)

GAY. All right. (THE WOMAN *moves.*) Why do you live? (*Her trolley stops.*)

OLD WOMAN. Out of habit. Why do you?

GAY. You are very impertinent for a thing on castors.

OLD WOMAN. Beg pardon —

GAY. What are you trying to make me do? Commit suicide?

OLD WOMAN. No, I just —

GAY. Isn't there enough suicide without you —

OLD WOMAN. All over the shop —

GAY. I could regard that question as an attempt on my life!

SECOND OFFICER. We'll bring charges —

GAY. No, get her out — (SECOND OFFICER *propels her.*) And see she's washed...! (*Pause.*)

SAVAGE. That was Helen...

GAY. Idiot.

SAVAGE. **Helen!**

GAY. Do you think I don't know my own mother...?

CHARITY. **I wish you wouldn't interrupt the book.** (GAY *and* THE OFFICERS *go out. Pause.*)

CHARITY. Chapter One! No! **Introduction.** (*She shuts her eyes.*) Ready. Expatiate!

CREUSA (*suddenly*). It's coming —

CHARITY. Shh!

CREUSA (*stands*). The child —

CHARITY. The book!

CREUSA. **The miracle! Savage!** (SAVAGE *jumps up.*)

CHARITY (*to* SAVAGE). If you go, you will never write the book. (*He hesitates.*) You know that, don't you? You do know that?

CREUSA. **The child, Savage...!** (*He stares, his mouth open.*)

CHARITY. 'This book was so nearly never written..'

MACLUBY (*entering*). Examining your feelings, Dr Savage?

CHARITY. 'So nearly never written because I pretended feelings I did not possess..'

MACLUBY. She only wants her hand held...

CHARITY. Conscience delays all journeys, but especially journeys of the mind... (*She jumps up.*) That's it, first line! (MACLUBY *assists* CREUSA *away.* SAVAGE *watches.*) Refusal. That's the only way we learn. (*A high wind.* SAVAGE *turns impulsively on* THE CHILD *and starts to throttle her. By a twisting motion of her body,* CHARITY *escapes.* SAVAGE *reels.* FLADDER *enters, carrying a rule, a yard long. He places it against a wall and makes a chalk line. He turns, sees* SAVAGE.)

FLADDER. That low. (*Pause.* SAVAGE *reassembles himself.*)

SAVAGE. What...

FLADDER. That low. (FLADDER *goes off.*)

Scene Six

Under the city gate. THE OLD WOMAN, *parked.*

CREUSA (*entering with a mass of bundles*). I did it.

OLD WOMAN. You did.

CREUSA. And it is whole.

OLD WOMAN. That's something all Troy knows.

CREUSA. Look, it feeds off me...its fingers reach for my flooding tit, which, as if to ridicule my age, is bursting. Sixty, and in surplus!

OLD WOMAN. Baldness and abundance. Arthritis and suck.

CREUSA. Don't wonder where these gifts come from...

OLD WOMAN. Enjoy your miracles and keep your mouth shut.

CREUSA (*hoisting her load*). Off now.

OLD WOMAN. And by the same gate, Creusa...! Forty years since you last fled. (*Pause.* CREUSA *looks at her.*)

CREUSA. By the same gate, yes.

OLD WOMAN. Good luck!

CREUSA. Some dithering old peasant will lend me a corner of his sack, and if he don't speak Trojan, all the better, spare me his preamble, and swop dinner simply for the fuck.

OLD WOMAN. No note for the husband?

CREUSA. Once a quitter, always a quitter. Tell him that.

OLD WOMAN. Damn all reconciliations. It couldn't last. They say he had been Helen's man, so really it never had a chance.

CREUSA. It wasn't that.

OLD WOMAN. Once tasted, Helen spoiled a man for others —

CREUSA. **It wasn't that.** (*Pause.*) He had no hope. (*Pause.*)

OLD WOMAN. Hope? Can you eat that? (CREUSA *shrugs, sets off.* FLADDER *enters with his rule and chalk. He marks a wall, is about to go.*) First Troy was burnt by foreigners. But last Troy the people burn themselves.

FLADDER. That low! (*He departs.*)

OLD WOMAN. What...! (THREE YOUTHS *are hustled in.* GAY *enters.*)

FIRST OFFICER. Three more who say they have seen Helen and enjoyed her!

GAY. Where?

FIRST YOUTH. Down the docks.

SECOND OFFICER. When?

FIRST YOUTH. Between seven and eleven, I don't know exactly, time stood still —

GAY. What did she say?

FIRST YOUTH. Nothing.

GAY. Nothing? Neither mm nor ahh?

FIRST YOUTH. She's dumb, ain't she? (*He looks to the others.*) Helen's dumb? (THE OFFICER *thrusts him away. He runs.*)

FIRST OFFICER. You!

SECOND YOUTH. I met her near the botanical gardens and she drew me in —

GAY. To what?

SECOND YOUTH. The lily house, we poured with sweat —

GAY. When?

SECOND YOUTH. Some time between — say, five and nine —

SECOND OFFICER. **Five and nine?**

SECOND YOUTH. I couldn't say exactly, time stood still —

FIRST OFFICER (*elbowing him away, addressing the next*). Where?

THIRD YOUTH. On a bus —

SECOND OFFICER. Upstairs or down —

THIRD YOUTH. Upstairs, of course

GAY. When?

THIRD YOUTH. Oh, anything between —

SECOND OFFICER. **Time stood still did it?**

THIRD YOUTH. Yer know! He knows, so why —

FIRST OFFICER. And is she dark or fair?

SECOND/THIRD. 'er 'ead is shaved! (*They laugh and run.*)

GAY. Someone is chalking lines. All over Troy, a metre high. Both on the villas and the slums.

SECOND OFFICER. Not some one Mrs. Some many have been caught with chalk.

OLD WOMAN. Where's the harm in a line?

GAY. We don't know, but we think it has a message.

OFFICER. There's one! (*He goes to the wall and taking out a cloth, begins rubbing* FLADDER'S *line.*)

GAY. And oddly, the suicides have ceased.

OLD WOMAN. That's good, if life is...

GAY. Not good! (*Pause. They look at her.*) No, not good, because the hate must go somewhere. The hatred must. If only we had Helen! She could be the object but now it's the state!

SECOND OFFICER (*seeing* A YOUTH *at a wall*). Oi! (*He grapples* THE YOUTH *to the floor.*)

GAY. Oh, hold him! He stinks of cellars! And don't puncture him! be careful of his blood!

SECOND OFFICER (*kneeling on* THE YOUTH). What's this with chalk?

GAY. His spit! Be careful, all their fluids kill!

SECOND OFFICER. What!

FOURTH YOUTH. That low —

SECOND OFFICER. Come again, you —

FOURTH YOUTH. **That — low —** (THE OFFICER *looks at* GAY.)

GAY. Release him.

SECOND OFFICER. Release him?

GAY. Kill him, then, what difference does it make? (*Pause.* THE OFFICER *kills* THE YOUTH. OTHER YOUTHS *pass, running.* SAVAGE *enters.*)

SAVAGE. The Miracle has gone.

GAY. Into the park with its —

SAVAGE. Been in the park. Just dogs. Just starlings. And dirty youths marking the trees with rules.

GAY. And the mother? Where is she?

SAVAGE. Gone. Without a note.

GAY. Deserted you? But she's seventy! (*A sound of disintegration.* FLAD-DER, *with* YOUTHS, *hurtles in. They stop.*)

FLADDER. **Last Troy.** (*Pause. She stares at him.*)

GAY. I understood — you — had — no — tongue —

FLADDER (*opening a cavernous mouth*). **No tongue.** (*She stares.*) But I articulate the people. (*A fall of buildings. He thrusts out the ruler.*) **That high.** The ruins. **That low.** The city. (*People pour out the city, with or without bundles.* THE OLD WOMAN *is buffetted.* FLADDER *departs in the surge of the crowd.*)

OLD WOMAN. Oi! Mind my trolley! (*She is knocked.*) That hurt, idiot! (*And trodden.*) Bite your arse! **What's the rush?** It's no different over the hill, I know because I been there! (*She shouts.*) **They built eleven Troys and every one was faulty! I loved eleven men and every one was flawed. But do I surrender?**

EPSOM (*passing with a sack*). Save yer breath, four wheels...

OLD WOMAN. Oh, my second father!

EPSOM. Ta ta, four stumps...

OLD WOMAN. Don't go, I still got lips —

EPSOM. Fuck it —

OLD WOMAN. Fuck it, yes, what's in the sack?

EPSOM (*departing*). Daggers.

OLD WOMAN. **Yer can't eat daggers.** (*He goes.*) Teach a man a trade, and he'll find hirers...

SAVAGE (*seeing*). Helen...

OLD WOMAN. Oi! My trolley! (*Some women start to tip her.*) Come off it, girls, steal from the wealthy if you must — rob yer enemies — (*They lift her off, dump her on the ground and place their bundles on the trolley.*) **Well, that's nothing if not predictable!** (*One slaps her.*) Sorry! Suffer in silence! Sorry!

SAVAGE. Helen...

OLD WOMAN (*now in the midst of the torrent*). Sorry — can't move...beg pardon... (*A sack is dropped, abandoned. Tablets of soap spill out over the ground.* THE OLD WOMAN *cranes to smell them.*) Hyacinth! I smell you, Hyacinth!

SAVAGE (*beside her*). It's you...

OLD WOMAN. No, it's not.

SAVAGE. It is...it's you...

OLD WOMAN. Not me. And never was. (*A shattering of masonry.*) No Helen but what other people made of her. I deny the body exists except within the compass of another's arms... (*A rush of fugitives.* CHARITY *glimpses* SAVAGE.)

CHARITY. Come on! We've not finished yet!

SAVAGE. No, nor started...

CHARITY. Chapter One! (*He stares at her.*) But I'm the book...! (*He doesn't move.* THE CROWD *moves on,* CHARITY *with them.*)

OLD WOMAN. Give us a lift, somebody! Give us a lift! (*She is spun round.*) I go in a pocket! I go in a bag! Oi! (*She is knocked onto her back. She lies, laughing.* THE CROWD *thins to individual scattering.*)

MACLUBY (*appearing with a sack into which he pops the soap tablets*). All gone except the cripples...

OLD WOMAN. 'ho are you calling a cripple? (*He looks at her with supreme detachment.*) I suppose if birds shit in my mouth I might be fed... (*She opens her mouth. Pause.*) Come on, sparrow, I chucked pastry at you once...from honeyed beds...from honeyed balconies...my fingers crumbled over-abundant cake... **Short memory!** (SAVAGE *looks at* THE OLD WOMAN. *He looks around him. Pause.* MACLUBY *tosses him a spade*

OLD WOMAN. Terrible shortage of sparrows...come on, pigeons, divest! (*She opens her mouth wider still.*) Crows? (SAVAGE *goes to her. He flings on a shovel of earth.*) Anyone! (*He flings on another.*) Oi! (*and another*) **I got no power, why must I be dead?** (*He smothers her with earth, breathless. She is silent. He walks back to* GAY, *flings the shovel at* MACLUBY. GAY *wraps* SAVAGE *in her arms. He is still.*)

SAVAGE. All that I know...and all you don't...

GAY. Shh...

SAVAGE. The long length of our quarrel yet to come...

GAY. Shh...

SAVAGE. Shallow reconciliations and lingering angers in the dark...

GAY. That's love, isn't it? (*He looks at her.*)

SAVAGE. Cut that short, then.

GAY. Love...hammered out thing...shapeless thing...

SAVAGE. Cut that short, then.

GAY. Bashed out like copper...warped like yew...

SAVAGE. **Cut that short, then.** (*She kisses him, but silently. He throttles her, letting her body lie over him. Pause. The wind.* THE BOY *enters, with a stiff bag. He looks at his father.*)

BOY. Find what you wanted?

SAVAGE. Thank you, yes... (THE BOY *turns to go.*) Kiss me...? (THE BOY *looks at him, blankly.*) All right, give us the plate! (THE BOY *looks puzzled*.) Broken plate...(SAVAGE *indicates with a nod the shards of broken plate which lie among the litter*. THE BOY *picks up a piece, gives it to him, goes*. SAVAGE *attempts to slash his own throat*.) Can't... (*He braces himself, but fails*.) **Can't!** (*and again*) **How did the old man do it? Can't!** (*He chucks down the shard*.)

MACLUBY. What do you think suicide is, a solitary act? It's peopled with absences.

SAVAGE. I have absences.

MACLUBY. You murdered everything, and long for nothing. Aren't you already dead? (*He picks up his bag and walks away*.)

SAVAGE. That's knowledge, then... (*Pause. Whistling offstage. ASAFIR enters, sees SAVAGE*.)

ASAFIR. Hey! We are having a picnic here.

SAVAGE. Don't mind me.

ASAFIR (*off*). Hey! (JOHN *enters, bowed by hampers*.) This is the picnic place.

YORAKIM (*entering*). Oh.

SAVAGE. Don't mind me.

ASAFIR. But this is a picnic place!

SCHLIEMANN (*as guide*). The University! What a terrible place this was! The little rooms suggestive of a gaol, the —

YORAKIM. Erm —

SCHLIEMANN. The corridors of inordinate length where tortured thinkers thrashed each other in pursuit of a deity they called Truth —

YORAKIM. Erm —

SCHLIEMANN. A deity without shape or form, of course, these were not primitives — (*He looks at* SAVAGE.) Are you on the tour? (*An inordinate pause. Black*.)